1988

Ada Louise Huxtable

The Tall Building Artistically Reconsidered:

The Search for a Skyscraper Style

Pantheon Books, New York

Portions of this book originally appeared,
in slightly different form, in *New Criterion*,
Volume 1, Number 3, November 1982.

Picture credits appear on page 122.

Library of Congress Cataloging in Publication Data:

Huxtable, Ada Louise.
    The tall building artistically reconsidered.
    Includes index.
1. Skyscrapers.   I. Title.
NA6230.H89 1984   725'.2   84–42664

ISBN 0–394–53773–4

Manufactured in the United States of America.

First Edition

Design: Massimo Vignelli.

This book on the skyscraper began as the Hitchcock lectures at the University of California at Berkeley in April of 1982. Under the sponsorship of the School of Environmental Studies and with the kind encouragement of Dean Richard Bender, I was able to pursue a single, century-spanning theme, the design development of the tall building. The approach, based on a long view—the 1880s to the 1980s—was basically a personal one; I have always been fascinated by the fact that the skyscraper, as architecture, is so much more than an account of the battle of its styles.

To deal with this spectacular phenomenon in the customary fashion—only in aesthetic terms, or as a purely technological development—is to misunderstand both architecture itself and the sources of its strengths and weaknesses, the difficult transitions from intent to reality, and the complex creative processes that turn necessity into art. These dynamics make for a tension and a provocative vitality that are particular characteristics of the building art. Beauty or beast, the modern skyscraper is a major force with a strong magnetic field. It draws into its physical being all of the factors that propel and characterize modern civilization. The skyscraper is the point where art and the city meet.

The privilege of the large or long view is not usually available to working journalists, who take history on a daily basis, building by building and blow by blow, nor do newspapers give academic sabbaticals for study and reflection. For the gift of time and freedom, I am indebted to the John D. and Catherine T. MacArthur Foundation; as a MacArthur Fellow I left the *New York Times* to embark on a renewed course of scholarship in which my most valuable resources are the accumulated information and experience of many years of involvement with architecture as art and process in its more pragmatic and immediate terms, and a reverence for the pursuit of facts learned doing research as a graduate student in architectural history.

Critics are not people blessed with sudden flashes of miraculous insight; they are not given to revelatory interpretation, like some saintly vision. The insights come when the facts all come together; they are the wonderful reward for the sifting and searching of first-hand material—a process that has its own pleasures in unexpected discoveries and uncharted trips through time. The flashy hypotheses and borrowed ideas fashionable in intellectual circles today are much less interesting than the far more remarkable and relevant items waiting in records and archives; the miracle, the moment of truth, is when these documents and drawings begin to reveal a picture as intriguing as it may be unfamiliar. Every generation tailors history to its taste. But for the look and feel of the artist's own work and words, of his own hand, and for what these things tell us directly, there is no substitute. The only way to know the past is to go there.

To be able to develop and refine a favorite theme, to feel one's comprehension grow even as one realizes how much more there is to learn, is a singular pleasure. There is no ultimate truth, of course; for history, and reality, many roads can be traveled; there are many perspectives from which the view of the past may be seen. By the time the Hitchcock lectures had become an article, at something like novella length, in the November 1982 issue of *The New Criterion,* my ideas had begun to come together more firmly. The lecture illustrations could not be used, and that was a loss, but for me, much understanding was gained through the reflection that accompanies the rewriting process. The stylistic vicissitudes of the tall building, which had customarily been treated selectively and fragmentally, seemed to mesh with a convincing clarity and continuity, when allowed to, almost by themselves.

Given the passage of time, of course, most history has a way of falling, or being pushed, into place, but this particularly fortuitous, or free-floating, moment between modernism and something called postmodernism seems to sharpen the eye and the mind; it suggests useful questions and encourages a freshness of perception for anyone who has not espoused any particular theory or joined any camp. As historian and critic, I value this independent and inquiring vision above everything else.

The two years that have passed since the initiation of this work and the publication of the article have resulted in substantial additions and changes that may not be immediately apparent. The opening exposition remains the same, now with pictorial evidence to support it visually. From midsection on, the text has been largely revised and contains much new material, with a fuller discussion of more architects and buildings. The timing has been fortunate; the preparation of the book has coincided with an explosion of new work and the first flowering of what can only be acknowledged as a new skyscraper age. Skylines are in radical flux. Many of the examples included were hot off the drawing board at publication time, and their impact continues to be startling. The new material not only updates the book, but adds considerably to its thesis. It is particularly gratifying to finally have the text and illustrations together. The book has been planned so that the pictures can be read, with their captions, as a kind of précis of the essay's arguments, while the text itself is meant to be illuminated by the examples shown.

As a native New Yorker, I should probably be sated with skylines by now. But I respond to the drama of the skyscraper like a first-time visitor to the big city; its stunning variety and awesome concentration make this one of the most exciting architecture stories ever told. These tall buildings embody the best, and the worst, of our times. The message is inescapable. And it is, of course, a cautionary tale.

Ada Louise Huxtable

New York City
October 1984

The skyscraper and the twentieth century are synonymous; the tall building is the landmark of our age. As a structural marvel that breaks the traditional limits on mankind's persistent ambition to build to the heavens, the skyscraper is this century's most stunning architectural phenomenon. It is certainly its most overwhelming architectural presence. Shaper of cities and fortunes, it is the dream, past and present, acknowledged or unacknowledged, of almost every architect. From the Tower of Babel onward, the fantasies of builders have been vertical rather than horizontal. Frank Lloyd Wright, caustic critic of cities, could still project a mile-high skyscraper; when the Futurists proclaimed an energetic new world, it was in the form of streamlined, soaring towers. These flamboyant visions, full of pride and prejudice, have released architectural talents and egos from the rule of reason and responsibility.

But the question of how to design the tall building has never really been resolved; it continues to plague, disconcert, and confound theorists and practitioners alike. The answers were first sought in models of the past, which were later rejected and then still later rediscovered, carrying reputations up and down with vertiginous regularity. At any point in the cycle, the arguments have an air of messianic conviction fueled by equal amounts of innocence and ignorance. In the final analysis, the results are controlled less by any calculated intent than by those subtle manipulators of art and ideas—taste, fashion, and status.

The cycles of taste and the evaluation of the product are complicated further by the fact that architecture, like other arts, has not been free from the ideological politics, cliques, and skillful and often venomous *ad hominem* attacks that are a curious and constant part of the art world. This fact has never been more obvious than it is in architecture today. There is a kind of guerrilla intellectual warfare operating from academia to the media, motivated by something that is unique to architecture—the direct connection between the bases of power and extremely lucrative work. Nowhere are the battle lines more clearly drawn than on the skyline. The modernist-postmodernist camps are in hand-to-hand, building-to-building, polemic-to-polemic combat on a huge scale, the postmodernists as intent on breaking rules and heads as on pursuing artistic frontiers. The script is familiar. Heroes are turned into villains, and the overthrow of the old regime is accompanied by the savaging of its leaders and the ravages of cultural revolution. The sound of smashing idols is everywhere.

All this is not news; the swings of art and taste are as certain as the seasons, and men with ideas who hope to change the world tend to behave no better than those who merely suffer the consequences. But in this contentious intellectual and artistic atmosphere, the skyscraper is being discussed and dissected with more intensity than at any time since the name was coined for the multistoried office building some time around 1890. The revisionists are busy rewriting history in terms of omission and rediscovery, which is fine, and they are also rewriting the rules of skyscraper design, which is not quite so acceptable or admirable. In the process, the right lessons are often discarded for the wrong ones.

In its most familiar and exhilarating aspect, the skyscraper has been a celebration of modern building technology. But it is just as much a product of zoning and tax law, the real-estate and money markets, code and client requirements, energy and aesthetics, politics and speculation. Not least is the fact that it is the biggest investment game in town.

With all of this, and often in spite of it, the skyscraper is still an art form. The tall building has that in common with all major works of architecture consciously conceived in aesthetic terms. Every radical advance or conservative retrenchment that has been proclaimed as the latest revelation of truth and beauty has actually been devoted to a single, unchanging, unifying idea and purpose: the search for a skyscraper style. The tall building has been designed well, and even brilliantly, in many different ways, and the exotic variety that marks the best of the tall buildings is inconsistent and irreconcilable in theoretical or doctrinaire terms. There are not, and never have been, any immutable rules; there is more than one way to skin a skyscraper. Contrary to accepted opinion and the respected critical texts, there have been many appropriate and legitimate responses to the conflicting cultural forces of our time.

This reality—the doctrine of irreconcilability—has never been accepted. We are edging toward it with talk of diversity and pluralism. As time passes and towers multiply, it is increasingly clear that skyscraper design has been motivated, above all, by an unresolved search for style, which is its only aesthetic consistency. No matter how revolutionary the rationale, how startling the claims of aesthetic breakthrough, how great the debt to advances in engineering, or how many times the old is discarded for the new, the objective has been the same. Proclamations of innovation and reform and protestations of use and suitability have all served the same end. That there has been this overriding, aesthetic preoccupation should not be surprising. Architecture is, admittedly, an extremely complex and pragmatic art, but it is an art nonetheless, and one which endures on its final quality. Only when a building transcends its inconvenient marriage of aesthetics and economics does it become convincing, and even great, architecture.

It is the rare architect who does not hope in his heart to design a great building and for whom the quest is not a quiet, consuming passion. Architects talk about little else to their peers; they seem obsessed with the aesthetic implication of their designs in word and print. A good deal less is said about this in the client boardroom, where the architect tells it not the way it is but the way it sells. There are some extraordinary reasons given for some extraordinary stylistic flourishes. But because architecture is a practical art, and practical men pay the bills, the search for style has been rationalized and camouflaged, not only to suit the prevailing intellectual fashion but to provide client reassurance that nothing so arcane is influencing efficiency and the financial bottom line. It is the singular architect, in fact, someone like Philip Johnson, who can walk in and tell corporate directors that they are getting art and get away with it. But in his case personality and product together constitute the art form.

The architecture of the tall building has never been more on people's minds, if one judges by public and press attention to the subject. Beyond aesthetics, however, there are serious questions of cause and effect, propriety and place, structure and style, that are not being addressed. There are pivotal issues of enormous importance to the design of the tall building, both subtle and complex, from the humanitarian to the historical, that need careful scrutiny. There is an incredible default of critical appraisal where it counts, and where it hurts, in the lives of cities and people.

The most obvious blind spot comes in the failure to recognize the fact that the skyscraper—still on the rise and increasing spectacularly in number and size—may have overreached itself, and may even be nearing the end of the line. There is both irony and tragedy in the realization that this is happening at the same time that the question of design has been creatively reopened by the loosening of modernist strictures, and at the mo-

ment when the exploration of the tall building's inherent power, drama, and beauty offers greater options than ever before. We are seeing some spectacular new building, but we are also seeing signs of a disturbing dead end in scale and impact, and a frivolous dead end in style. While the aesthetic debate becomes more recondite and self-serving, the effect of the tall building on our overcrowded, malfunctioning, and deteriorating cities has become demonstrably destructive and dehumanizing.

Today architects are looking at some very big buildings in some very small ways. The larger the structure, the less inclination there seems to be to come to grips with the complexities of its condition and the dilemma it creates. It is no longer considered necessary to look beyond the street facade. The examples of history, respectable again after half a century of denial, are being mined for nostalgia, novelty, and innuendo. But history should teach reasonable and profound lessons about the uses of style; it should not be used to supply obscure allusions or decorative ready-mades. An increasingly limited preoccupation with surface appears to be coupled with a sheer, stubborn disregard for the people and the cities the structures serve. The awe and wonder that architects first felt about the technological breakthrough and the new aesthetic options of the tall building, and their expressed desire to integrate these innovations into the social and urban fabric, have been replaced by a very narrow vision in which formal effect, fashion, and obsessive self-expression are overriding concerns.

One does not expect the larger contextual vision from builders and bankers, for whom investment is primary. But one does expect it from architects, as part of a responsible design process. Certainly we have long passed the point where anyone believes that the architect can solve the ills of society or remake the environment, or even that he should try. But there is still a responsibility to incorporate into design solutions thoughtful considerations of the real world and humanistic and environmental values and goals that go beyond scenographic fun and games. If the architect has erred in the past by claiming powers beyond his art, he has now reversed himself and is diminishing that art. He has no one to blame but himself if he finally makes his work seem marginal. The latest aesthetic trend seems to be toward a kind of monster picturesqueness, an approach that subverts and denies the real scope and purpose of building. If it is possible to trivialize anything as large as the skyscraper, that process is taking place now. This default of intent and meaning diminishes all architecture in a very real sense.

But the most immediate casualty has been in critical standards of judgment. What is lost in the emphasis on architecture for art's sake are broad, objective criteria by which all styles and approaches must properly be judged. These are the enduring principles that relate the problem to the solution: the creative fusion of struc-

ture and appearance in the service of utility and profit that has informed the best tall buildings.

That these principles of skyscraper design are being attacked as part of the well-publicized rejection of modern architecture is deeply disturbing, because they have been thought about carefully and well during the last hundred years, and they have a lot going for them as the appropriate and sometimes inspired translation of technology and market forces into art. A successful skyscraper solution, and the art of architecture itself, depend on how well the structural, utilitarian, environmental, and public roles of the tall building are resolved. Style—any style—must be intrinsic to, and expressive of, these considerations. Architecture is, above all, an expressive art.

The success or failure of a building is ultimately measured by how well these factors have coalesced into a unified, expressive whole. When the result adds a special dimension to personal and urban experience, when that expressive object forever transforms the concept or vision of the environment, when it alters the popular received image, it is proper to say that a major architectural contribution has been made. The proof, of course, is that after certain buildings have appeared— the Parthenon, the Pazzi Chapel, the Villa Savoie—the world has been altered in a subtle and substantial way; cities never look the same again.

Surely that is true of the tall building; the skyscraper has totally changed the scale and appearance and concept of cities and the perceptions of people in them. The public has always loved these architectural aberrations—like freaks of all kinds. The title of the world's tallest building has a fleeting but special cachet; it is a favored setting for publicity stunts and self-celebrations, media events, and cinema mythology. But if the status and drama of the tall building, its engineering and architectural achievements, its embodiment of superlatives, are universally admired, the philosophical questions that it raises continue to be disturbing: its symbolism is complex, its role in the life of the city and the individual is vexing, and its impact is shattering. The skyscraper is Olympian or Orwellian, depending on how you look at it.

For the skyscraper is not only the building of the century, it is also the single work of architecture that can be studied as the embodiment and expression of much that makes the century what it is. Today's tall building is a puzzling and paradoxical package. Its standardized, characterless, impersonal space creates the recognizable, charismatic monuments and the enduring image of twentieth-century cities. For better or for worse, it is measure, parameter, or apotheosis of our consumer and corporate culture. No other building type incorporates so many of the forces of the modern world, or has been so expressive of changing belief systems and so responsive to changing tastes and practices. It romanticizes power and the urban condition and celebrates leverage and cash flow. Its less romantic side

effects are greed and chaos writ monstrously large. The tall building probes our collective psyche as it probes the sky.

In sum, the skyscraper—in terms of size, structure, and function, scale and symbolism, and, above all, human and urban impact—remains the single most challenging design problem of our time. The other definitive architectural challenge, housing, will continue to lack patronage and priorities because it answers to social rather than to business needs. The twentieth-century architect's most telling and lasting response to his age is the topless tower of trade.

The tall building today is also an enormous and cautionary symbol of the changes taking place at a rapid rate in the philosophy and practice of architecture—changes that have not only transformed the look of buildings but have polarized the profession. It serves as both standard-bearer and whipping-boy for modernists and postmodernists of every persuasion. Today's skyscraper stands at a crossroads between a new and an old vision—between architecture as mission and architecture as style—in one of the most significant transitional periods in the history of art.

Louis Sullivan, whose early skyscraper solutions have still not been surpassed, discussed its aesthetic and philosophical aspects in an 1896 article called "The Tall Office Building Artistically Considered." Like the tall building itself, the essay is an uneasy synthesis of poetry and logic. But the questions Sullivan raised about the design of the tall building remain pertinent, unsettled—and unsettling—today. They are, in fact, more pressing than ever.

I have entitled this essay *The Tall Building Artistically Reconsidered* in homage to Sullivan, and because I believe the time has come for a critical reevaluation beyond what is currently passing by that name. The history of the skyscraper to date is incomplete and misleading. Like a Rashomon account, it has been told from a number of restricted and subjective points of view which still need to be brought together in a unified whole. Until now, the perception of the design development of the tall building has been tailored to suit those who have made taste and written history in this highly polemical century. We have the brilliant, insightful, but carefully selective version by Sigfried Giedion, in the mainstream of modernist doctrine. Winston Weisman's researches have dealt authoritatively with definition and chronology. The technology of the skyscraper has been thoroughly documented by Carl Condit. But the omissions are as important as the inclusions, and the story is just beginning to be rewritten, along with much nineteenth- and twentieth-century history. The result, however, is a new kind of imbalance that may be the normal price of radical revisionism, and even with the gaps being filled distortions continue. If the architectural deck has been stacked unfairly in the past, it is being shuffled and restacked just as erroneously now, with the "outs" replacing the "ins" and one set of preferences, or prejudices, being substituted for another.

Revising Skyscraper History

Aesthetic interpretations of the design of the tall building have always absorbed architects and critics. But the basic questions remain the same. How does one clothe the new, naked skeleton? How can one fit this attenuated giant into existing architectural conventions? How will it relate to a setting totally alien to its scale, structure, and use? The answers, then as now, have evolved as much from temperament as from art. From the start there were the conservatives who were sure that the only safe, sanctified solutions must touch base with tradition, and the radicals who believed that a leap of faith into the future must be made through a brave break with the past. Today, curiously enough, those roles have been reversed. Radicalism is represented by a respect for the past that was outlawed by the modern movement, a return to sources appearing in a number of idiosyncratic guises, while conservatism is marked by an adherence to the doctrine of established modernism.

By the turn of the century, the distinguished architecture critic Montgomery Schuyler was calling openly for "aberrations." It was the "deviation from the customary structure or type," he said, that would break new ground. Schuyler repeatedly attacked formulas derived from historical precedent as baseless or arbitrary; they followed assumptions that were true for masonry, he said, but false and obsolete for steel. The results were not solutions, in his reasoning, but evasions of the real nature and problem of the modern office building.

A more representative and conventional viewpoint was offered to the thirty-third convention of the American Institute of Architects meeting in Pittsburgh in 1899. In a paper called "The Legitimate Design of the Architectural Casing for Steel Skeleton Structures," a respected turn-of-the-century practitioner, Clarence H. Blackall, asked: "Should we break away from the precedents of the past . . . ?" The answer, he said, "involves a consideration of what constitutes legitimate design. Illegitimacy, as we well know, is defined as unrecognized parentage. . . . The most truly legitimate of all architectural design is the one which has survived, in its various modifications, through the wreck of the Roman Empire, the untoward influences of the Vandals and the Goths, and has come to us still intact in spirit after all scathing modern episodes. . . . We are safer following pretty closely the line of Classic architecture and Italian Renaissance," he concluded, "and there is more hope for a good copy than there is for a bad original." So much for aberrations.

What Schuyler was attacking and Blackall was defending at that time was the increasingly popular idea that the tall building should be treated as a classical column, an analogy that yielded a tripartite division into base, shaft, and capital. To Schuyler this was the kind of "arbitrary assumption" that could "obstruct the detailed expression in design of structure and function." But it had enormous appeal for Beaux Arts–trained practitioners, and for all those who subscribed to the popular Aristotelian principle that a work of art should have a beginning, a middle, and an end. It evoked the mysteries of trinities in nature. It suggested golden proportions and the beauties of organic form. Blackall referred to the work of Louis Sullivan with faint praise and little sympathy as the "extreme impressionistic school." To Schuyler, Sullivan's buildings were the admirable aberrations that broke new ground. Sullivan himself, in "The Tall Office Building Artistically Considered," took issue with the classicists. "Form ever follows function," he wrote in a famous statement that has since been stripped and sanitized of all of Sullivan's lyricism by the literalness of later generations. He spoke not of classical analogies but of the intrinsic and expressive relationships of form and structure in nature and in art.

Looking at the whole historical spectrum of skyscraper design, we can identify four significant phases: the functional, the eclectic, the modern, and the postmodern—the last more descriptive of the state of mind of its practitioners than of any real success in cutting the modernist umbilical cord. It is significant that all of the most important structural solutions came early in the development of the tall building, in a remarkably

The history of the skyscraper falls into four significant phases, or styles: functional, eclectic, modern, and postmodern. The early, or functional, skyscraper was an economic phenomenon; business was the engine that drove innovation. The patron was the investment banker and the muse was cost-efficiency; architecture was the servant of engineering, and design was tied to the bottom line. These buildings are as handsome as they are utilitarian. They have a clarity and strength that gives them remarkable expressive power.

1

1. *Monadnock Block, Chicago. Burnham and Root, 1889–91.*
2. *Republic building, Chicago. Holabird and Roche, 1905–09. Demolished 1961.*
3. *Reliance building, Chicago. C. B. Atwood of Burnham and Company, 1894.*

2

3

The second, or eclectic, phase produced some of the sky-scraper's most remarkable monuments. Raids on the past ranged from banal to brilliant: the Gothic reached for the heavens as never before; mega-Greek temples and neo-Italian campanili, stretch-Renaissance palazzi and zoom-châteaux were adapted with ingenuity and skill, bringing occasional real beauty to the twentieth-century city.

1

1. Temple Court, New York, Sillmian and Farnsworth, 1882–83, 1889–90; Woolworth building, New York, Cass Gilbert, 1913.
2. Standard Oil building, New York. Carrère and Hastings, and Shreve, Lamb, and Blake, 1922.
3. Liberty tower, New York. Henry Ives Cobb, 1909.

2

3

The modernists endorsed sweeping revolution in everything from art to the human condition; the modern skyscraper was seen as a creative challenge requiring an original response to technological and cultural change. This yielded a stringent structural aesthetic of deceptive simplicity capable of a suave and distinctive elegance.

1

1. Lever House, New York. Gordon Bunshaft of Skidmore, Owings, and Merrill, 1952.
2. Federal Center, Chicago. Mies van der Rohe, 1956–65.
3. Inland Steel, Chicago. Skidmore, Owings, and Merrill, 1954.

2

3

19

The postmodern skyscraper is a building of overwhelming scale and impact. The loosening of modernist strictures and the exploration of the tall building's inherent power and drama offer greater options than ever before. History, respectable again, is being mined for nostalgia, novelty, and innuendo. At best, these buildings flirt with new frontiers; at worst, they offer a monumentally frivolous dead end.

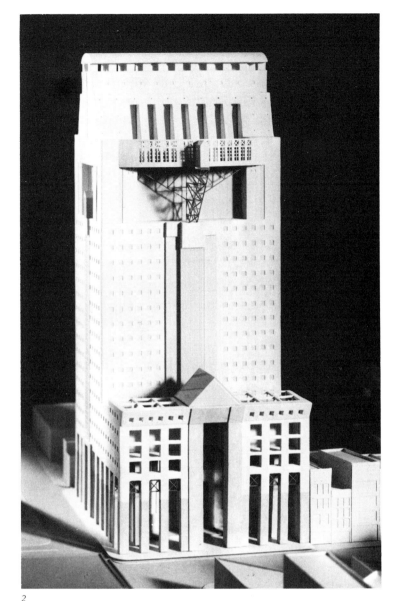

2

3

1.   *AT&T building, New York. Johnson, Burgee, 1978–83. Model.*

2.   *Humana, Inc., headquarters, Louisville. Michael Graves, 1982–84. Model.*

3.   *Project for Northwestern Terminal building, Chicago. Murphy, Jahn, 1981. Drawing.*

short space of time. Because these structures were concentrated in Chicago in the two decades at the end of the last century, other burgeoning cities quickly acknowledged the "Chicago style" in their commercial construction.

It has been customary, or one might say mandatory, in the right art-history circles to draw a straight line from this early Chicago School to the fully developed modernism of the twentieth century, dismissing everything in between as unacceptable architectural behavior. This has consigned a large body of significant work to a kind of limbo. As a result, both our perception of the time frame within which important stylistic changes occurred and our evaluation of their worth has been faulty and self-serving. The eclectic and modern phases —or modernist, as the latter is now called—were actually of about the same duration, and both lasted much longer than the initial period of innovation. There was a significant, unacknowledged overlap, with the modern phase moving into ascendancy only after the Second World War.

The modernist skyscraper, however, has been endorsed by scholars and critics in terms of an "authenticity" that the eclectic work has been denied. That is a defensible, if currently unpopular, position. Style is creative change in response to cultural change; it is the way in which that culture expresses the conditions of a particular society and time. This creative process inevitably produces the most original and interesting results. Defining the creative force in these terms has worked very well for the rest of art history. An innovative talent will engage the imagination more than a polished practitioner of tradition, even when the experiments are flawed or the conventions are impeccable. It is the uneven frontiers of creativity, with their disturbing and energizing combination of brilliant insights and inevitable judgmental errors, that reveal new aspects of humanity and the physical world and map new aesthetic territory.

The problem of those buildings that espoused classical or Gothic or Renaissance sources over *"l'esprit nouveau"* or "form follows function" is that they muddied the radical modernist line. The idea of aesthetic coexistence had no meaning at all for the theorists of the early twentieth century, who were single-mindedly focused on sweeping revolution in everything from art to the human condition. We are only beginning to understand and accept the artistic and cultural complexity of a century that has been vastly oversimplified. We are shortchanging our own art when we deny its contrasts and contradictions. The search for consistency and conviction is one way of trying to pull back from the threat of chaos and the loss of traditional beliefs and values that characterize our time. And we fail to come to terms with the difficult meanings of this turbulence when we dismiss it with the bland put-down and cop-out of undifferentiated "pluralism."

The skyscraper was a response to the growth of cities and business and the concentration of commercial activities housing many people on increasingly congested and expensive urban sites. Its most dramatic technological advance was the quickly erected metal frame and curtain wall. The nonsupporting exterior facade could be clad at any point; it was no longer restricted to rising slowly and weightily from the ground. This was a subject for both scientific and popular notice. It was this novel feature of the New York Life building, constructed in Chicago by Jenney and Mundie, that was illustrated in the American Architect and Building News *of February 10, 1894.*

The First Skyscraper Age

Except for popular mythology and a totemic fascination with the skyscraper, its history has been too narrowly focused. There is general agreement on the significance of certain structures and events, such as those innovations that had their roots in many places and flowered in Chicago in the late nineteenth century. At that time, and in that place, a unique combination of industrialization, business, and real estate came together for the development of a new and distinctive building type: the American office building.

In the first, or what might be called the functional, phase of this new structural phenomenon, architecture was the servant of engineering. Rapid increases in building height were made possible by advances in fireproofing, metal framing, and the passenger elevator, as well as by less glamorous improvements in footings and foundations, plumbing, heating, lighting, and ventilation. Much larger buildings were encouraged by the rapid erection of the metal frame and curtain wall, the growth of cities and business, and the need and desire to house commercial operations that employed many people on increasingly congested and expensive urban sites. Essentially, the early skyscraper was an economic phenomenon in which business was the engine that drove innovation. The patron was the investment banker and the muse was cost-efficiency. Design was tied to the business equation, and style was secondary to the primary factors of investment and use.

The structural systems devised were simple and replicable. Aesthetic considerations became a subordinate function of the profitable development of land encouraged by advances in steel manufacture, skeleton construction, and mechanical services. No one was concerned with landmarks, or milestones, or icons, beyond the obvious identification of profit and prestige—least of all, with the stylistic resolution of a new building type. The priorities of the men who put up these buildings were economy, efficiency, size, and speed. With the later emphasis on artificial light and climate control —both a function of cheap American energy—all serious limitations were eventually removed from how big the building could be and the way it could be designed.

The pragmatism that controlled this first phase of the American skyscraper is usually laid to the philistinism and hard-nosed economic practices of the late-nineteenth-century Midwestern entrepreneur. But enthusiasm for the new Chicago buildings was shared by bankers and businessmen from the cultural centers of the Eastern establishment, who also knew a good thing when they saw it. The builders of one of Chicago's most distinguished early commercial landmarks, Burnham and Root's Monadnock Block of 1889–91, were Peter and Shephard Brooks of Boston.

A revealing quotation, from a letter of May 6, 1894, written by Peter Charndon Brooks to Owen Aldis, the Chicago lawyer who managed the Brookses' Chicago real estate, has been sent to me by John Coolidge. The Monadnock Block was built with interior metal framing and masonry bearing walls, a type of transitional construction favored for a while over the skeleton frame and curtain wall, as it was thought to be more fireproof. The building has been noted for the simplicity of its smooth, flat surfaces, its monumental silhouette, and the subtly battered and color-graded walls that substitute for ornament.

One assumes that the instructions given to Aldis found their way to the architects, Burnham and Root. "My opinion," Brooks wrote, "is to have no projecting surfaces or indentations, but to have everything flush or flat or smooth with the walls—projections mean dirt, nor do they add strength to the building. . . . One great nuisance is the lodgement of pigeons and sparrows." This was hardly a mandate for high art. But these purely practical considerations were turned into a satisfactory aesthetic by the architects in an extreme but fairly representative demonstration of the role restrictive provisions can play in the shaping of a creative architectural solution.

Other impressive buildings came out of equally pragmatic requirements. The famous Chicago window —a three-part, projecting bay that created the extremely lively, plastic facades of structures like the Tacoma and Reliance buildings of 1889 and 1890 and Adler and Sullivan's old Stock Exchange of 1893–94—was a device to capture as much light and space as possible for the purpose of increasing the rental value of the

The early skyscraper enclosed the skeleton frame in the least costly fashion; its design features came out of pragmatic requirements. The handsome "Chicago window" was a device to capture space and light, thus increasing the rental value of the offices.

offices. For most builders, there was minimal interest in dressing up the new curtain walls; the idea was to enclose the skeleton frame in the least costly fashion.

Is it a paradox that these buildings—dictated overwhelmingly by economics and expediency—have been recognized and admired internationally as superior architectural achievements? Chicago is a favorite pilgrimage point for European architects of all generations. A talented group of younger, native practitioners is intensely aware of the city's early skyscraper history. The Chicago firm of Booth, Hansen, and Associates, designing a moderately tall building, looks to its architectural origins, rather ambitiously seeking "the quality of Root and Sullivan . . . organic structure, allegory to nature, and an American character." There is a conscious attempt today to build on, and in, the Chicago tradition.

These early structures are as handsome as they are utilitarian. They possess a great strength and clarity that gives them remarkable expressive power. We are as pleased by their art as their builders were by their technology. But we can also see that it is precisely the linkage between the two—art and technology—that is the secret of their distinctive and superior style.

In 1931, the building generally believed to be the first example of true skyscraper construction was demolished in Chicago. The Home Insurance building of 1884–85, by William LeBaron Jenney, was dismantled with great care by a special investigating committee of

1.   *Reliance building, Chicago. C. B. Atwood of Burnham and Company, 1894.*
2.   *Old Stock Exchange, Chicago. Adler and Sullivan, 1893. Demolished 1971.*

the Marshall Field estate, which determined that the building's claims of fathering the modern city were true; a metal skeleton frame supported both its inner weight and outer walls. That fact ascertained, the first building to reach for the sky bit the dust to make way for another—a gesture in the true Chicago spirit. From the Home Insurance building on, the height and appearance of the tall building were to be controlled only by engineering ingenuity, economic formulas, and personal ambition.

The Second Skyscraper Age

But the design debate about the skyscraper's artistic problems grew as quickly as its size, and soon led to the invocation of traditional models. The second phase of skyscraper design sought solutions through academic sources and historical precedents. This eclectic phase, which was fueled by the ascendance of the Academy and the popularity of the Beaux Arts in this country, continued well into the twentieth century, until both debate and construction were stopped by the Great Depression.

The eclectic phase produced some of the skyscraper's most remarkable monuments. The raids on the past ranged from banal to brilliant: the Gothic reached for the heavens as never before; Greek temples and Italian campanili raised their heads repeatedly in the sky. There were stretch-Renaissance-palazzi, zoom-châteaux, and assorted versions of the Mausoleum of Halicarnassus.

The size and style of these buildings made them spectacular and recognizable monuments, but their unique and unreproducible features are their sophisticated scholarship and superbly executed detail. The best examples were skilled academic exercises adapted with great ingenuity, drama, and, occasionally, real beauty to the totally new needs and aspirations of the twentieth-century city. Although the élite position has been to act as if they are, at best, pardonable eccentricities or, at worst, giant blots on the skyscape, they took their place instantly in the history of architecture.

The modernists have always read the academic victory as an architectural defeat. The characteristic of the eclectic phase that seemed like the cardinal architectural sin was not that its practitioners failed to seek new forms, which was bad enough, but that they placed such heavy emphasis on romantic recall and ornamental embellishment. After a long, austere diet of rationalism, however, younger architects are again delighting in this exotic and exuberant excess, and even an older generation is seeing these buildings with new eyes.

The tall building that was considered an exemplar of the eclectic mode at the end of the nineteenth century was Bruce Price's American Surety building of 1894–96 in New York. Its classical, tripartite division was widely discussed and approved, and it easily drew as much attention as a trend-setter as some of today's

But the design debate about the skyscraper grew as quickly as its size. From the start, the question of style absorbed architects; most looked to familiar sources for inspiration and answers. A tripartite division based on the classical column— base, shaft, and capital—was a widely accepted solution. Bruce Price's American Surety building in New York, constructed from 1894 to 1896, was upheld as an exemplar.

more eccentric towers. It is still a substantial and handsome structure, recycled in 1975 by the Bank of Tokyo.

The American Surety building followed another well-publicized New York example, George B. Post's Produce Exchange of 1883–84, which was being completed at the same time that Jenney's Home Insurance building was going up in Chicago. The Produce Exchange was a horizontal rather than a vertical building, but we are told by Carl Condit that Post may have used a true skeleton for the trading room slightly in advance of Jenney's landmark. Post himself claimed that only New York's building code, which required twelve-inch-thick walls in the 1880s, kept him from using curtain walls throughout.

The Exchange's exterior walls were impressively stylish, however; they would have horrified Peter Brooks. Tiered arcades of dark-red Philadelphia pressed brick were embellished with terra-cotta medallions of appropriate character—corn, cows, and pigs between forty-five-foot arches representing the original thirteen states. This blend of patriotism and pragmatism was supposed to take its aesthetic cues from Sansovino; the building was called, at the time, "modified Italian Renaissance" or "Venetian Roman-Gothic."

Critical opinion about the Produce Exchange was divided; it was hailed as "an object of permanent beauty" and derided as an "incarnation of sumach." The historian Talbot Hamlin later judged the building the best of Post's work, "striking in color . . . powerful

in design . . . expressive of its time." The Produce Exchange was a curious hybrid, a kind of Yankee Doodle Beaux Arts, but it was a wonderfully strong design—a typically unabashed combination of American technology and vigorously plundered European sources. When it was demolished in 1957 the job required a full arsenal of bulldozer, jackhammer, and wrecking ball, and revealed cast-iron columns, wrought-iron beams, and tie-rods of structural steel. The successor at 2 Broadway, a legitimate descendant if one considers only the engineering drawings, looks as if it could be demolished with a can opener.

In 1894, when Price's American Surety building was still in the design stage, a study directed to the resolution of the artistic problems of the new, tall office building was published by the respected and widely followed architectural periodical, the *American Architect and Building News.* The project was carried out by John Moser, a Fellow of the American Institute of Architects, who was commended by the author of the article for "honestly and manfully [approaching] the problem from the constructive side . . . as a necessity of modern life." Moser's avowed purpose was "to express, not hide or falsify, our incomparable modern steel construction, so that anyone, at a glance, may see how it is built, and so feel that it is strong and majestic." (Majestic is not a word or an idea that anyone has quite had the courage to revive overtly in an egalitarian, pluralistic society.) But the architect's "expressive

George B. Post's building for the New York Produce Exchange had already combined radical technology and stylistic ingenuity in the 1880s. An unabashed marriage of American innovation and vigorously plundered European sources, it was a strong and fashionable "Renaissance" design. Demolished in 1954, this impressive structure was replaced in 1959 by 2 Broadway, by Emery Roth and Sons. This skyscraper is the legitimate technological heir of the earlier building, but style is conspicuous by its absence.

honesty" led, surprisingly, backwards. "After the most mature consideration," he wrote, "I found myself getting very close to the Classic."

The building illustrated was divided into three sections suggesting the base, shaft, and capital of a classical column, an approach widely endorsed at the time as the most valid artistic solution of the problem. The pilasters with which a large number of floors were embraced, Moser admitted, gave him trouble, but his solution was, indeed, manful. "I pierced them," he explained, "bases, caps and all, the spaces between them being pierced with windows, [and] dressed them up with as agreeable forms as possible." In order to keep the twenty-story building from looking "attenuated," and to decrease the emphasis on its height, he topped it with a cornice heavy enough to sink a battleship.

Having created an elaborate, heavy-handed, and leaden mass singularly lacking in expressive grace, Moser offered a curiously contradictory prediction: "The office building of the future will be useful and practical," he wrote. "It will tell exactly what it is and pretend to be nothing else. . . . It will be elegant by virtue of its proportions, its refined simplicity and a skillful handling of its few ornamental forms."

What this described precisely, if with no intention of doing so, was the work of Louis Sullivan, who had fulfilled the prophecy by 1900. In the 1890s, Sullivan produced a series of masterful, original tall buildings, at first with his partner, Dankmar Adler, and later

The "artistic problem" of skyscraper design was addressed by the American Architect and Building News *of December 8, 1894. In a specially commissioned study, architect John Moser proposed an elaborate, elephantine version of "Classic" inspiration. At the same time that he produced a drawing of a heavy-handed, leaden mass in tortured pursuit of a "majestic" solution, he made a prediction of paradoxical prescience. The "office building of the future will be useful and practical," he said; "it will tell us what it is and nothing else."*

alone, that created what everyone was looking for: a skyscraper style. Running as a countercurrent to the rushing rivers of eclecticism was Sullivan's less-than-popular insistence that form followed function, not academic precedent. He believed that the design of the skyscraper was the creative translation of structure and plan into appropriate cladding and ornament, and that the answers were not to be found in the rules and practice of the past.

The Wainwright building of 1890–91 in St. Louis, the Guaranty building of 1894–95 in Buffalo, and the Carson, Pirie, Scott store of 1899–1901 in Chicago are among those structures that tell you exactly what they are. They are consummately elegant by virtue of Moser's own criteria: their proportions, the simplicity and clarity of those relationships of structure and enclosure, and the skilled use of an extraordinary ornament. Far from deemphasizing their height with academic stolidity, Sullivan delighted in celebrating their "loftiness," although they no longer seem high to us now. The tall building was not to be brought down to earth, he said, in another famous quotation; it was to be "a proud and soaring thing."

To this task, in the words of historian and critic Henry-Russell Hitchcock, Sullivan brought "a full, subtle deployment of architectural resources." The rational simplicity of the early Chicago School had not ever been lost. But Sullivan carried the solution of the tall building to a more thoughtful and sensitive level

1

The problem that so many were struggling with in print and in practice had already been solved by Louis Sullivan. Translating structure and plan into appropriate form, cladding, and ornament, without dependence on the rules and practice of the past, he had developed what others still sought: a skyscraper style.

1. *The Guaranty building, Buffalo. 1894–95.*
2. *Carson, Pirie, Scott store, Chicago. 1899–1901.*

2

Sullivan's Bayard building in New York, built 1897–99, was praised by the critic Montgomery Schuyler as a building that "tells its own story," based on "the facts of the case. . . . This is the thing itself." Sullivan's synthesis of the scientific and the aesthetic raised those facts to art.

of interpretation and embellishment, and a much more sophisticated kind of design. Montgomery Schuyler, in *The Skyscraper Up-to-Date,* used Sullivan's Bayard building of 1897–99 as an example of successful and appropriate tall-building design. The Bayard, originally the Condict building, still stands on Bleecker Street in New York, its lower floors mutilated but the whole enduringly handsome. It has been renovated and advertised as "Louis Sullivan's only building in New York" after years of dingy, marginal existence.

"Everywhere the drapery of clay is a mere wrapping," Schuyler wrote when the Bayard building was new, "which clings so closely to the frame as to reveal it, and even to emphasize it. The actual structure is left, or, rather, is helped, to tell its own story. It is an attempt, and a very serious attempt, to found the architecture of a tall building upon the facts of the case. This is the thing itself." The decoration, Schuyler noted, was of a quality no other designer could have commanded, "and is responsible for much of the building's aesthetic as distinguished from its scientific attractiveness." But it is the quality of the whole—that blend of the scientific and the aesthetic—that Schuyler understood and that few designers have commanded as well. Sullivan raised the "facts of the case"—which so distinguished the early Chicago skyscraper—to the status of art.

Louis Sullivan's achievement has never been discredited, but it has been misunderstood. The modernists looked at his work with a selective bias, carefully misreading his intentions, blind to the facts of the case. They accepted his science and rejected his aesthetics. They could never come to terms with his florid romanticism, and the lusher his ornament, the more they averted their eyes. That ornament was not anachronistic or out of place in Sullivan's own work or time, but it was incompatible with the modernists' attempts to reshape history and art to their purified revolutionary doctrines. Sullivan reserved his aesthetic options for subtler and more traditional things—the horizontal or vertical emphasis of the structural frame, for example —often achieving a delicate and remarkable equilibrium reflecting the kind of visual and visceral balance of which art is made. But his designs were admired by the modernists only according to how literally, or "truthfully," their construction was revealed. He was denied his poetic license.

Sullivan was a difficult case, because no matter how much his critics condemned what they considered his decorative backsliding, the logic, beauty, and originality of his solution was always clear. Like the modernists, he dismissed academic sources. In "The Tall Office Building Artistically Considered" he warned that the skyscraper should not "be made a field for the display of architectural knowledge in the encyclopedic sense." But while he rejected the idea of historical models, he did not deny the traditional architectural values and relationships of the decorated form.

Sullivan's highly personal search was soon eclipsed by the academic avalanche. The successful eclectic skyscraper, however, never actually violated Sullivan's insistence that form follows function in the broader sense, or Schuyler's conviction that the design of the tall building must be founded on the facts of the case. These structures take learned liberties, but they are still recognizable as the thing itself. Their indulgence is academic, rather than poetic, license. Cass Gilbert's French Renaissance 1905 building on West Street and Gothic Woolworth building of 1913, both in New York, state the facts of the case with superb visual richness and a masterful handling of the special problems of unprecedented size. These and other examples deal, if not directly, at least metaphorically and ornamentally, with the difficult realities of structure and scale. Style, whatever its source, was used as an instrument for dramatizing the facts of the case.

By 1922, the famous international competition for the Chicago Tribune tower demonstrated the full strength and range of the eclectic phase. This competition, which called for "the most beautiful and distinctive office building in the world" and drew more than two hundred submissions from twenty-three countries, was one of those benchmark events in the arts: it crystallized a unique moment in architecture when the long classical tradition was poised on the edge of the unknown abyss of modernism. The entries were a

1

Sullivan's highly personal search was soon buried by the academic avalanche. But the successful eclectic skyscraper never violated his, and Schuyler's, belief that the tall building should be founded on the facts of the case. Although these eclectic skyscrapers take learned liberties, they deal, metaphorically and ornamentally, with the difficult realities of structure and scale. Style is an instrument for dramatizing the facts of the case.

1.   90 West Street, New York. Cass Gilbert. 1905.

2

3

2. *Woolworth building, New York. Cass Gilbert, 1913.*
3. *Metropolitan Life tower, New York. Napoleon Le Brun, 1909.*
4. *Old New York Evening Post building, New York. Robert D. Kohn, 1906.*

4

In 1922, the international competition for the Chicago Tribune tower demonstrated the full strength and variety of the eclectic skyscraper. The range of entries, from avant-garde to retardataire, documents the state of the art of the tall building at the end of the first quarter of the twentieth century. These buildings crystallize a unique moment in architecture when the long classical tradition was poised on the edge of the unknown abyss of modernism. Massing, scale, and detail were well understood in any number of guises. What seemed improbable at that moment was that modernism would supplant eclecticism in another twenty-five years.

1. *First-prize design by Howells and Hood, United States.*
2. *Second-prize design by Eliel Saarinen, Finland.*
3. *Third-prize design by Holabird and Roche, United States.*
4. *Entry by Adolf Loos, Austria.*
5. *Entry by Walter Gropius, Germany.*

2

3

4

5

6

startling mix of the adventurous and the *retardataire,* but what is particularly interesting is that so many of the designs were so very good; the massing, scale, and detail of the tall building were well understood in any number of guises.

The subsequent bitter debate between those who championed the Gothic revival of the winning tower by Howells and Hood against the romantic Finnish modernism of Eliel Saarinen's second-prize design or the radical modernism of Walter Gropius's submission from the Bauhaus seems, in perspective, quite beside the point. Just as provocative today, and also impressive, are such less-familiar entries as a surprising number of Dutch examples that fall stylistically between Berlage and De Stijl. There were even submissions of a type now called "commentary," for example Adolf Loos's enormous classical column, which could have been conscious, or unconscious, irony; for all we know —and some scholar surely does know, or will (for one recent version, see Gravagnuolo Benedetto's "The 'Chicago Tribune' Column," an essay in *Adolf Loos,* published by Rizzoli in 1982)—he may have been playing it straight.

The Third Skyscraper Age
The Tribune tower competition has been held up by the modernists as a sad and ludicrous example of what went wrong with skyscraper design after Sullivan—a fall from aesthetic grace. From today's perspective,

however, it forms a remarkably accurate historical document of the state of the art of the skyscraper at the end of the first quarter of the twentieth century. What seemed improbable at that moment was that modernism was to supplant eclecticism as the architecture of the establishment in another twenty-five years. But the rout of tradition and the acceptance of the new was neither quick nor clear; the course of true modernism did not run as smoothly as historians have chosen to relate. Until recently, it has been inadmissible in proper intellectual and artistic circles to point out that there was a "modern-modernistic" dichotomy rather than the direct revolutionary line to which all the faithful immediately adhered. The conventional and respectable architectural wisdom has treated this conflict as a split between good and bad design, between serious and frivolous art, between aesthetic enlightenment and vestigial, uncomprehending vulgarity—in short, between virtue and sin.

The modern phase of skyscraper design actually embraced this dual aesthetic in two separate but parallel strains. "Modern" was radical, reductive, and reformist; "modernistic" was richly decorative and attached to conservative and hedonistic values. "Modern" was the austere, abstract, élite, avant-garde work of the European school of Gropius, Mies, and Le Corbusier, united in its early days under the rubric of the International Style. "Modernistic" was neither pure nor revolutionary; it fused the ornamental and the

6. *Entry by Bijvoet and Duiker, the Netherlands.*

Modernism came slowly to architecture, and in two versions: modern and modernistic. "Modern" was the austere, avant-garde, revolutionary International Style, which became the favored style of the commercial and cultural establishment by midcentury.

1. Project for a glass skyscraper, Friedrichstrasse, Berlin. Ludwig Mies van der Rohe, 1919. Drawing.
2. Seagram building, New York. Mies van der Rohe with Philip C. Johnson, 1954–58.
3. Civic Center, Chicago. Jacques Brownson of C. F. Murphy, with Skidmore, Owings, and Merrill and Loebl, Schlossman, and Bennett, 1963–68.
4. 140 Broadway, New York. Gordon Bunshaft of Skidmore, Owings, and Merrill, 1968.

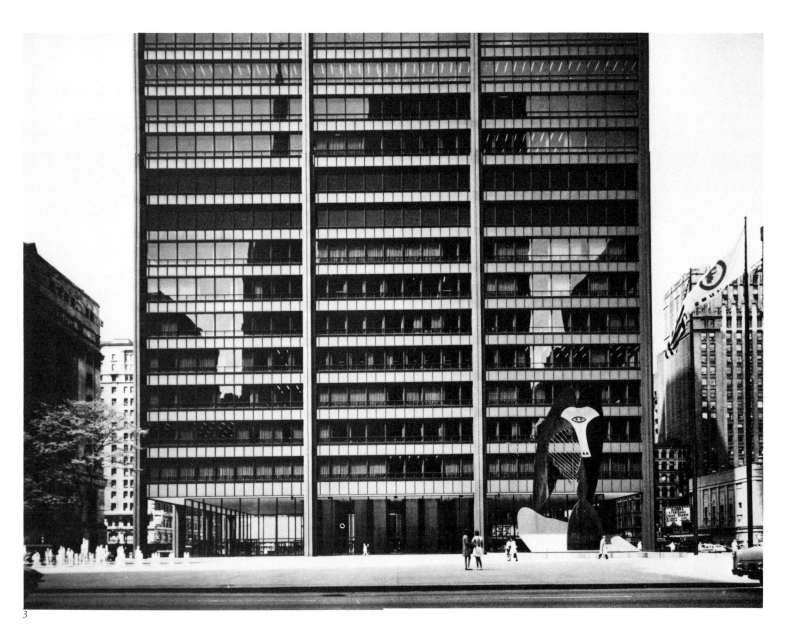

3

4

1

"Modernistic," more traditional and conservative, fused the ornamental and the exotic for the last of the great decorative arts. Some of the century's most seductive skyscrapers are modernistic.

2

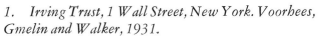

1. *Irving Trust, 1 Wall Street, New York. Voorhees, Gmelin and Walker, 1931.*
2. *Project for hotel. Holabird and Roche, c. 1930. Drawing.*
3. *Chanin building, New York. Sloan and Robertson, 1929.*
4. *60 Hudson Street, New York. Voorhees, Gmelin, and Walker, 1930.*
5. *Chrysler building, New York. William Van Alen, 1930.*

One celebrated skyscraper, the Daily News building of 1930, designed by Howells and Hood, fell between modern and modernistic, disturbing those who prefer ideological tidiness.

exotic for what was really the last great decorative style. Derived from the luxurious, exotic combination of new and old materials and the traditional fine craftsmanship that characterized the products of the 1925 Paris Exposition des Arts Decoratives et Industrielles, "modernistic" was despised by the avant-garde as fussy, reactionary, and, of course, bourgeois-decadent. Now called Art Moderne or Deco, it is having a trendy revival, but "modernistic" was the name used at the time—innocently by its admirers and scathingly by its critics. The modern-modernistic split was more than style-deep, however; the reformers saw modern as both moral and beautiful; it held the promise of a better world through design. They considered the more fashionable modernistic as the betrayal of that promise and the denial of art as an instrument of social change.

Some of the century's most seductive skyscrapers are modernistic, including Holabird and Root's very beautiful drawings of executed and unexecuted work in Chicago, and a number of pre-Crash towers in New York's financial district. Others, like Howells and Hood's New York Daily News building of 1930, fell between modern and modernistic, confounding the critics, who prefer ideological tidiness. The style died with the Depression, when construction stopped after the completion of the Chrysler and Empire State buildings in 1930 and 1931. Rockefeller Center was its protracted swan song, and although the complex's modernistic detailing and debt to Beaux Arts planning were ritually deplored until recently, this superior piece of urban design has taught important lessons about cities and style that are now universally acknowledged.

"True" modernism was pioneered by a handful of adherents to the radical, reductive International Style and its other European equivalents in the 1920s. Its scope and history are still little known or understood in this country, where it arrived in a bowdlerized and amputated form in the famous Museum of Modern Art "Modern Architecture" show organized by Henry-Russell Hitchcock and Philip Johnson in 1932 and in their enormously influential book, *The International Style.*

A far better book, in retrospect, was Hitchcock's earlier *Modern Architecture, Romanticism and Reintegration,* of 1929, in which the young scholar wrote perceptively of the two coexisting strains of European modernism as "The New Tradition" and "The New Pioneers." The catalogue of the museum's 1932 show, *Modern Architecture, International Exhibition,* covered the same ground as the Hitchcock and Johnson book on *The International Style,* with a slightly different cast of characters. Frank Lloyd Wright, for example, was included in the show and catalogue, with his presence explained by his influence on the Dutch modernist, J. J. P. Oud. Both museum publications were highly selective and restricted accounts that stripped the work of any social content or cultural context. "Sociology" was acknowledged as a separate section on "Housing" by Lewis Mumford, at the end—clearly a divorce of convenience and conviction.

Very little was built in the new International Style in the United States. While there was a large body of significant work abroad dating from the period just after World War I, only small, token structures appeared here, quite late, in the 1930s. At first, modernism was a showcase style of the avant-garde. Much later, in an even greater transformation, it became the architecture of the establishment. By midcentury, the revolutionary ideal and aesthetic had been turned into slick, profitable formulas that had lost an enormous amount in the translation from the European originals to American commercial practice.

The leaders of early European modernism rank high among the creative minds and talents of our time. Their artistic stature has much to do with the quality, importance, and influence of their work, and of the modern movement itself. In the final analysis, this will make the position of modernism stubbornly resistant to even the most assiduous downgrading. The process of denial and devaluation, taking place now, ranges from the critical trashing of modernism to the proposition that the whole modernist episode is an expendable error and absurd digression that disrupted architectural traditions within which cultural meanings and metaphors were well established and successfully in place. The fact that the twentieth century had already disrupted those meanings beyond restitution is ignored or glossed over. The attempt to restore them relies on glib superficialities of formal rhetoric—the papering-over of a totally different cultural reality with classical or vernacular cut-and-paste is surely one of the most limited intellectual and aesthetic exercises in the complex history of the building art.

If the obsessive and monumental vision of the early modernists was to lead to serious consequences, it was a vision that grew out of an extraordinary moment in human history. We know now that the moment, and the spirit, were delusory. But the illusion that the sentinel towers of the ideal future would replace the confused and chaotic past in born-again cities, and that the past, with its errors, would not be missed, was cherished by otherwise reasonable men. Part of the illusion was that the renewal of the city and the spirit would come through the miracle of mass-produced technology.

This was a time of which the distinguished linguist Roman Jacobson, who was also a participant in the excitement of the Russian revolution in the arts and literature, could write in wonder, many years later, "We threw ourselves toward the future with too much passion and avidity to be able to retain a past. The ligature of time was torn. We lived too much for the future, thought of it too much, believed in it, we no longer had the sensation of an actuality that was sufficient unto itself, we lost the feeling for the present." Although this visionary detachment encouraged the brilliant exploration of creative ideas, it led to the problem that has scarred our cities and the century—the affectless context in which the new buildings were conceived; they were meant to exist in shining and exemplary isolation. To dismiss the achievements of modernism with its failures, however, is like discarding the plays of Shakespeare for their bowdlerized versions and bad performances. There is no belittling the period's exploratory dynamism and the definitive extension of conceptual and aesthetic boundaries. Modernism will also have its revisionist historians.

It is indisputable now that this vision was tragically flawed—that modern architecture aimed too high and promised too much, in defiance of too many natural laws. As with so much else, a naïve and generous optimism and faith in the creative and therapeutic powers of art gave way to a disillusioned cynicism and reactive pragmatism that has been characteristic of this century, conditioned by the cataclysmic changes that destroyed more than artistic ideals.

The early modern, or International Style, skyscrapers are few in number; they required clients with cash, courage, and a highly developed sense of aesthetic mission. Theoretically, the combination of form and function these buildings endorsed was supposed to be beyond style; actually, style was their most enduring product. The McGraw-Hill building of 1931, constructed in midtown Manhattan by Hood, Godley and Fouilhoux, is a notable example, and the Philadelphia

1

2

The early modern, or International Style, skyscrapers are few in number. Their combination of form and function was supposed to be beyond style, but style was their most enduring product.

1.   McGraw-Hill building, New York. Hood, Godley, and Fouilhoux, 1931.
2.   Philadelphia Savings Fund Society building, Philadelphia. Howe and Lescaze, 1930–31.

Savings Fund Society building of 1930–31, by Howe and Lescaze, is a total work of art. The descendants of these buildings are the largely unloved flattops and glass boxes—relieved by an occasional modern masterpiece—that make up the High Modern Corporate style. This is the look that has shaped the skyline of the twentieth-century city. Not all those who took up the cause of modern art in the 1920s were International Style party-liners. The influential critic Lewis Mumford expressed his opinions in some memorable columns in the *New Yorker* and the *Architectural Record.* In 1928, he defined the new modern architecture in an *Architectural Record* article called "The Search for Something More." A building should be "the direct, economical expression of material and plan," he wrote. "The clear, lucid expression . . . of form-in-function is what constitutes the modern feeling." But, he added, going beyond the ritual revolutionary declarations, "there must be something more." That "something more" he described as a combination of structure and feeling. "It is by utilizing new methods of construction and embodying a new feeling that our modern architecture lives," and it is over the question of what this "something more" must consist "that the new battle of the styles will be fought."

Significantly, Mumford's "something more" included ornament. Decoration was no "snare and smear" for him, as it was for others; he had generous words for such buildings as Ely Jacques Kahn's new skyscraper at Two Park Avenue with its brightly colored bands of geometric terra-cotta ornament, praising its integration of mass and decoration as "the boldest and clearest note among all our recent achievements in skyscraper architecture. . . . [Here] structure and feeling are at last one." But the battle of the styles that Mumford expected was never fought in the terms he anticipated. The search for "something more" became "less is more" by mid-century. When business and technology met in extraordinary conjunction in American cities after World War II, the architecture of this latest marriage of convenience—pragmatic, cost-cutting, market-oriented, riding the wave of a business boom—had interesting parallels with the first Chicago School. By one of those odd and fateful coincidences of art history, the modernism of "less is more" was also a simple and replicable style ideally suited for commercial use on a large scale. If its socioaesthetic ideals proved unrealizable, its design principles were ready-made for economic exploitation. Developers were able to knock them off with the same skill and profit with which they manipulated land and law. These big buildings have taught us hard lessons. They range from the corruption of art and ideas to unprecedented problems in the construction of cities. Such problems, however, owe as much to investment patterns and social upheaval as to aesthetic decisions. But the minimalism of the modernist aesthetic lends itself to a subtle, ascetic beauty or to the cheapest corner-cutting; and since the latter has been the easiest

Some critics called for "something more" than the austerities of the International Style. In 1928, Lewis Mumford praised Ely Jacques Kahn's new skyscraper at 2 Park Avenue for its integration of mass, ornament, and color.

and most profitable route for the builder, an elegant, reductive vocabulary was quickly reduced to a bottom-line banality that its creators never dreamed of. Unfortunately, the loss was of exactly that critical quality of detail, material, and execution on which the modern style depends.

For the uncorrupted source of this brand of modernism one must go back to the pioneer tall-building projects by Ludwig Mies van der Rohe in Berlin just after World War I. Anyone who denies the significance or splendor of Mies's seminal designs for the skyscraper not only fails to see these buildings as they were conceived but also seriously shortchanges art and history. A particular aesthetic vision is a function of a particular time and place—but this work still transcends both. The prismatic glass tower scheme of 1919 for the Friedrich-strasse, always shown in abstract isolation, is as responsive to its site as to an ideal vision; the curved glass tower project of 1920–21 is a consummate aesthetic statement of intent and ideal. Here is the quintessential twentieth-century tension between art and technology, between dream and reality; these tall buildings sum up the architectural drama and beauty and the innovative genius of our time. Structure in its most pure and perfect form was enclosed in a sheer curtain of shaped and shimmering glass for a breathtakingly transparent geometry—a concept inseparable from the developments in technology that made it a creative possibility.

Reality, however, never delivers the dream. This breathtaking, skin-and-bones abstraction, this stringent equation of beauty and technique, was an unreachable objective. Mies was a great enough artist to come close a number of times; he produced buildings of sustained art and elegance. But like Sullivan, Mies has been much misunderstood. It has been popular to point knowingly to piers that never reach the ground and corner details that deliberately short-circuit literal structural truth as evidence that his functionalism was faulty, and as proof positive of the betrayal of modernism's avowed principles. Today's critics are quick to attack the fallacy of his search for universal solutions; his ideal space and modular systems are seen, ironically, as a hopeless Procrustean bed. Clearly, a narrow functionalism was never his intent; what he provided was structural symbolism as a high art form for a technological age. He is denied his poetic license.

The offspring of those two Mies drawings are legion. The standard for quality and consistency was set by the work of the firm of Skidmore, Owings, and Merrill, which became the chief interpreter of the Miesian aesthetic and the most prestigious practitioner of the High Modern Corporate style. These are the skyscrapers of the Fortune 500—suave, skilled variations on the themes of structural rationalism, machine-age luxury, and institutional status. They are the buildings that symbolize the state of the skyscraper art at midcentury —a quarter-century after the Chicago Tribune tower

1

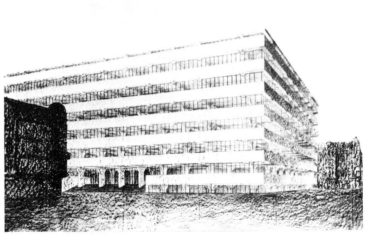

2

3

4

By the end of World War II, "something more" had become "less is more." The midcentury corporate skyscraper brought business and technology together in a pragmatic, cost-effective way that paralleled the early Chicago School. The standard for star corporate clients and consistent commercial quality was set by the firm of Skidmore, Owings, and Merrill. All of these buildings go back to the seminal designs of Mies van der Rohe.

1. Curved glass skyscraper project. Mies van der Rohe, 1920–21. Drawing.
2. Project for reinforced concrete office building. Mies van der Rohe, 1922. Drawing.
3. Union Carbide building, New York. Walter Severinghaus of Skidmore, Owings, and Merrill, 1957–60.
4. Sears tower, Chicago. Bruce Graham and Fazlur Khan of Skidmore, Owings, and Merrill, 1970–74.

competition—and in the decades that followed. These skyscrapers are long on understated splendor and structural panache, and short on poetic license.

But if the lyricism was lost, a vernacular was gained. I have never shared the view of critics who claim that the glass box is an icy curse visited upon us by the distortion of Mies's "failed" vision. The failed vision is theirs. The Miesian skyscraper is the basis of a superb vernacular, probably the handsomest and most useful set of architectural conventions since the Georgian row house. Its rejection is unrealistic. To accept the vernacular of the suburban strip and reject the urban vernacular is ludicrous, particularly since this establishes a double standard, or value system, when all value judgments have been declared unacceptable.

The Miesian aesthetic has produced an eminently suitable twentieth-century vernacular style for this century's unique and overpowering scale—a fact that has yet to be fully realized or appreciated by critics or historians. Vernacular art grows out of the high art of the time and is applied to its common needs and purposes. As with all vernacular architecture, it is the standardization and anonymity of forms reduced to a rational, useful simplicity—here the sleek, reflective surfaces and facets of glass, mirror, and metal—that have universal application and appeal. The result is as right for today's skyscraper cities as Georgian detail was for the scale and purposes of the eighteenth century. This vernacular accommodates the inhuman size,

The Miesian aesthetic has produced a twentieth-century
vernacular style that is singularly suitable for the modern
city's unique and overpowering scale. This vernacular—as
right for the modern metropolis as the Georgian was for the
eighteenth-century city—accommodates today's inhuman size,
mass, and bulk with an appropriate and saving simplicity.
Glass towers may reflect many of the defects of the society
they serve, but their aesthetic mix of substance and reflection
makes a magnificent street architecture.

mass, and bulk that are the inescapable facts of life and architecture with an appropriate and saving simplicity. Glass towers, whatever their drawbacks—and most of their faults are independent of aesthetics—make a magnificent street architecture.

Moving Beyond Modernism

While business and builders were busy exploiting the modern style, another more subtle kind of exploitation was being carried out by the architects themselves. Straining at the straitjacket of rigid modernist principles, while giving lip service to them, they found ways to stretch the rules. The sacred dictum that form follows function was being turned into the pursuit of form for its own sake. Structure became sculpture; sometimes the whole building was transformed into a sculptural or decorative object. Or it was conceived as a provocative, abstract play of light, planes, and reflections, a trick done with mirrors, as the glass box gave way to the mirror-glass building, a development of considerable aesthetic subtlety and intricacy. The modern skyscraper, once devoted to a Euclidian simplicity, began to display a far more complex geometry. Very quietly, the rules of rational cause and effect were reversed, and structure became a tool for creating abstract, idiosyncratic, and arbitrary results. Function followed form. Less became quite a lot more. The avenues explored ranged from macho contortions to sophisticated experiments aimed at the expansion or exploitation of

the traditional relationships of function and form. From Stamford, Connecticut, to Paris's La Défense, new commercial developments began to look like a structural muscle beach. For better or worse, architects were clearly moving into a new phase of design.

In the best of these transitional skyscrapers, Schuyler's "scientific" and "aesthetic" criteria and Mumford's "structure and feeling" were, and are, still working together. We are able to see and understand and marvel at the synthesis of structure and style in these designs, and even the deliberate bravura with which one controls the other; there can be enormous architectural power in the way technical components are manipulated for aesthetic effect. This, too, is poetic license, but it is never unrelated to the facts of the case.

Some of the most successful of these explorations were carried out early by Philip Johnson, always the leader in the search for the new, before he moved on to a questionable historicism. (It is not the historicism one questions but the architectural results.) The IDS tower of 1968–73 in Minneapolis and the Pennzoil building of 1976 in Houston, both the work of the Johnson, Burgee firm, pointed the way to structures that fused outer form and inner space in a most suggestive way; they were in the vanguard of a new skyscraper aesthetic. The United Nations Plaza Hotel by Kevin Roche of Roche, Dinkeloo was completed in New York in the same year that Pennzoil changed the Houston skyline. Roche's 1976 design uses mirrored surfaces and unexpected angles to play on, and with, the visual effects of scale and light for a less-than-simple set of signals belied by the unbroken surface sleekness. At the same time, I. M. Pei was embracing circles and ovals, as well as angles, but these new shapes were used in the classic modernist sense of "pure" form, not as decorative departures; they sent simple, mono-lithic messages rather than complex or contradictory ones. Pei's curved tower for the Oversea-Chinese Banking Corporation in Singapore also dates from 1976.

Harry Weese, one of Chicago's well-established modernists, began to explore structural principles and novel shapes in departures aimed at the supertall building meant to break the 100- or even the 200-story barrier. The enduring modernist firm of Skidmore, Owings, and Merrill increasingly folded and faceted its elegant boxes; its engineers also forged ahead with the invention of a "superframe," following the successful "bundled-tube" construction of the record-setting, 110-story Sears tower in Chicago in 1974. Cesar Pelli, who has studiously avoided the sensational, continued to work within a consistent set of architectural values, stretching but never abandoning the basic relationships between physical cause and aesthetic effect. But even his concisely controlled rationalism moved into an equally controlled romanticism in a 1983 design for a pinnacled office tower in New Orleans.

Paul Rudolph's vigorously articulated buildings have always invoked a complex interplay of plan and

1

The modern skyscraper, once devoted to a Euclidean simplicity, began to display a far more complex geometry as architects struggled against the rigid limitations of modernist principles. Immense skills have been invested in enlarging structural and aesthetic options within these restrictions, for striking exercises in sculptural shape and scale. Function frequently follows form, and less has turned into quite a bit more.

1. *Pennzoil building, Houston, Texas. Johnson, Burgee, 1976.*

2

3

2. *United Nations Plaza Hotel, New York. Roche, Dinkeloo, 1976.*
3. *3 First National Plaza, Chicago. Skidmore, Owings, and Merrill, 1978–81.*
4. *Oversea-Chinese Banking Corporation Center, Singapore. I. M. Pei and Partners, 1976.*
5. *101 Park Avenue, New York. Eli Attia Architects, 1979–81.*

4

5

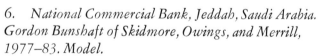

6. *National Commercial Bank, Jeddah, Saudi Arabia.*
Gordon Bunshaft of Skidmore, Owings, and Merrill,
1977–83. Model.
7. *Project for skyscraper. Harry Weese and Associates,*
1981. Model.
8. *City Center, Fort Worth. Paul Rudolph, 1983–84.*
9. *Project for office tower, New Orleans. Cesar Pelli and*
Associates, 1983. Model.

9

elevation reflected in their dynamic exteriors. Breaking accepted canons of modernist taste and practice in the 1960s, these interlocking "megastructures," shell-like spirals and cascades of inner space, were often met with confusion and rejection. The Yale Art and Architecture building of 1966 became a symbol of that decade's student rebellion—the designer's intent and the building's interior spaces were systematically trashed as a revolt against imposed order and functional deficiencies at a time when chaos was elevated to a state of grace. But the building's idiosyncracies also evoked the wrathful denunciation of the great modernist critic, Nikolaus Pevsner, who considered its artful intricacies a frivolous retreat.

With hindsight, it is clear that Rudolph had a head start into what has come to be perceived as postmodern expressionism. The constructivist massing of his twin towers for the Fort Worth city center, completed in 1984, no longer seems surprising; what is evident is their aesthetically assured and effective handling. Mirror glass helped make them à la mode. But this is a proto-postmodernist language that Rudolph had been speaking instinctively for some time, like the prose of Molière's bourgeois gentilhomme.

The apotheosis of late modernist geometry is one of the most extraordinary structures of the 1970s— Gordon Bunshaft's design for the National Commercial Bank in Jeddah, Saudi Arabia, executed before he retired from Skidmore, Owings, and Merrill. This building takes modernism, at full, formalist tilt, to a brilliant conceptual limit. The scale is not only enormous, it is also unreadable. The smooth, unbroken masonry walls, closed against the sun, are pierced by three large inward-turned openings at ascending levels of the triangular shaft; these "stacked atriums" give no hint of the building's real scale or size, or even of its human use. From a distance, it is as mute as the pyramids. The floor levels and the design module can be read only on the structure's glazed interior. This masterful tour de force breaks all expected or perceived relationships with a building's setting or function; Bunshaft's powerful, formalist manipulation has created the ultimate object-monument. Modernism can go no farther on the course set by its American sponsors in 1932. It has come a very long way from the model espoused by the social and aesthetic revolutionaries that gave birth to the International Style.

In 1974, Arthur Drexler, director of the Department of Architecture and Design at the Museum of Modern Art, dedicated a large exhibition to some of the more dramatic distortions of the facts of the case. Called "Transformations in Modern Architecture," it demonstrated how a once radical, functionalist rationale had been warped into a new and disturbing emphasis on form for its own, and only, sake. The show's most unsettling aspect was that no judgments were made; all examples, from reasonable investigations to pointless exhibitionism, were shown as a seamless iconographical phenomenon, and there was a high quotient of the perfectly awful. The practitioners of postmodernism were relegated to a fringe position. The exhibition was a massive indictment of formalism at the same time that it seemed to display a perverse delight in some of its more dreadful aspects; it managed to offend architects of every persuasion.

What is clear now is that from the 1960s on, the stylistic dicta of modernism were being manipulated to ever greater extremes, until they finally approached a point of rupture where the rules no longer held at all. The debasement of Mies's elegant minimalism was bearing a bitter and boring fruit; commercial abuse had reached a point of terminal mediocrity. The sins of modernism are many, as any reader of popular books and articles on the failures of modern architecture must know, but the real crisis, and the final, unforgivable sin, was the loss of style.

The Fourth Skyscraper Age

Together, these factors have led to a new phase of tall-building design, matched by an explosion of towers in totally new guises. Larger and more numerous than ever before, they are changing the American skyline radically once again. This development is marked by some extraordinary advances in technological expertise, in ironic conjunction with one of the most antistructural approaches to design in building history—the stylistic phenomenon known as postmodernism.

The most conspicuous and questionable characteristic of postmodernism is the renunciation and devaluation of everything the modernists believed in and built —a not-unexpected event to anyone familiar with the history of changing values and institutions, from art to politics. Its most encouraging aspects are the rediscovery of the past and the continuum and context of the city, and the recognition of the values of diversity. The postmodernists want everything back that the modernists discarded—history, ornament, context, contrast, variety, symbolism, imagery, and metaphor. And they are off pursuing these things, like Stephen Leacock's legendary horseman, in every direction at once.

Above all, postmodernism is a freewheeling, unfettered, and unapologetic exploration of style. The fact that style is paramount, beyond all other expressed concerns and aspirations, is the source of both its strengths and its weaknesses. The exploration of style can, and does, enlarge the boundaries of art. But in architecture it also creates a special danger: style detached from the conditions and considerations upon which the art of building rests can reduce architecture to something less than its proper role and definition, including its best practice and necessary attachment to reality. This emphasis not only affects the use and value of architecture to society; it ultimately and tragically diminishes it as an art.

Assessments of modernist failure, deserved and undeserved, have been used as the springboard out of the old and into the new, and as justification for the renunciation of the sociological and planning commitments of earlier generations. There are no forbidden routes to style for the postmodernists; everything, past and present, is looked at from the limited perspective of style, and everything is seen as a legitimate source of design. Today's architects are busy overcompensating for decades of sensory deprivation. But above all, they are preoccupied with making reputations and images. For many, it is no longer considered important, or even necessary, to relate those images to the facts of the case.

Newly discovered historical sources are used for a personal and idiosyncratic isolation of stylish elements. Bits and pieces of architectural history are detached from their context and meaning to serve as independent vehicles of ideas or decoration, something that tends to work much better in theory than in practice. The range of interpretive reuse of the past is wide. Postmodern classicism, for example, can embrace anything from a return to literate and literal Palladianism to the dreamlike montages of historical fragments that form the private architectural mythology of Michael Graves.

Revisionist taste runs to the elevation of new heroes, preferably those brutally deposed by the modern movement, and to the rediscovery of periods and practitioners that were declared the enemies of art by its leaders. The unfashionable and the unspeakable are suddenly in vogue. The emphasis on the masterful and often witty academic designs for government buildings, banks, and stately homes that Edwin Lutyens produced for the British establishment in the early years of this century, as one instance, has become notably obsessive, although some valuable studies have resulted. This highly arbitrary return to history, inadequately digested and often purposefully misconstrued, is commonly coupled with a warped and disingenuous view of the sins and errors of the modern movement, which, in any event, is considered foolishly misguided and hopelessly old-hat.

This process only repeats history, of course; the modernists' well-publicized lack of esteem and understanding for the Victorian age led to the uncomprehending loss of many of its monuments and documents, and to the difficult problems of assessment and appreciation that face scholars now. That same danger is very real and disheartening for the survival of the monuments and documents of the twentieth century. In each case, the earlier period is seen as a total dereliction of art and taste. There are those who now call modernism an aberration, an unfortunate and deplorable deflection of tradition that put architecture off course for most of this century. In this argument, Louis Kahn, for example, could have stayed with his Beaux Arts training and spared himself, and us, his struggles to define architecture in epochal and transcendental terms. What a loss for art that would have been! For those who are more concerned with history than with polemics, or perhaps one should say the history of

polemics, the significance of the present transitional moment is marred by the sabotage of self-serving short-sightedness.

One interesting and insidious aspect of the postmodernists' use of the past is a current phenomenon that goes considerably beyond its architectural manifestation. Today's preferred styles are more than the customary reversals of taste. They seem to express a social and political neoconservatism that goes beyond the admiration of more conventional and traditional aesthetic values to a kind of longing for the traditional social order and practices those values have served. This attitude runs from simple nostalgia for a more gracious and well-embellished era to something somewhat nastier—a parvenu old-tie, antiliberal snobbism of the new, and young, far Right. But postmodern radicalism is an odd creature; its practitioners tend to be architectural monarchists, regardless of background or training, with the customary preference for cake over bread.

The New Eclecticism

The conventional name for a selective historicism is eclecticism; but this new eclecticism is not the orderly selection of elements from different styles and systems according to the established academic rules that marked its practice in the past. The new version of eclecticism is personal rather than institutional, to the point of being private, hermetic, and maverick all the way. The acknowledged leader of the skyscraper division of this kind of postmodern eclecticism is Philip Johnson, a man whose social and aesthetic credentials are impeccable and whose mercurial pursuit of a fast-moving avant-garde keeps the profession on its toes—or at least off balance—much of the time. His own work has moved from the sculptural abstraction of the IDS building in Minneapolis and Pennzoil in Houston to a picturesque eclecticism in which absolutely anything that can be copied or adapted goes, as long as it offers a constantly changing spectrum of sensations to an extraordinarily keen, responsive, and easily bored sensibility and mind. It must also be able to be blown up instantly to skyscraper scale.

The Johnson, Burgee firm (in the early 1980s, the firm's name was changed to John Burgee Architects with Philip Johnson) offers a wide choice in its skyscraper line. The controversial Chippendale model for AT&T in New York, which made the cover of *Time,* putting architecture on the media map, was followed by medieval battlements in Lower Manhattan, a pinnacled, mirror-Gothic highrise for PPG Industries in Pittsburgh, and a modernistic cylindrical tower in San Francisco. An occasional excess, like a turreted castle for New York's Madison Avenue, has been aborted, but the product has been popular, nationwide. These buildings trip lightly from style to style. Houston has the firm's Art Deco Transco tower and the new RepublicBank headquarters in the guise of a giant gingerbread guild hall. Clearly, the surface of history has only begun to be scratched.

If the sources are diverse, the results suffer from a certain sameness; rarely do these eclectic exercises coalesce into an architectural statement with the authority of the examples so blithely exploited. Their so-called playful use of history is heavy-handed; their paper-thin pretensions misfire, no matter how solidly enclosed or dazzlingly surfaced. But they do carry a message; their failure to capture the architectural importance that they aspire to through the use of samples and swatches selected at random from history is a demonstration of the essential and inescapable relationship between art and its generating forces, from structure to society. However, if cleverness can substitute for this confluence of formative factors, then these buildings are simply not clever enough. The problem is not that they fail to say the same thing as the buildings they crib from—that is neither possible in today's world nor their avowed intention—it is that they say nothing at all. The dumb but reasonably honest glass box at least has the virtue of a saving simplicity; there is no virtue in elaborate vacuity.

It becomes a point of wonder that such respected architectural devices as the arcades and oculi of the AT&T building, with the enormously exaggerated scale of the structure's traditionally composed base, shaft, and top, can result in anything so flaccid and so unexceptional as this assemblage of painstakingly and

1

Postmodernism is a freewheeling, unfettered, and unapologetic pursuit of style. Certainly there are no longer any
rules or forbidden routes. In the skyscraper division of postmodern eclecticism, Philip Johnson is the acknowledged
leader. The Johnson, Burgee collaboration has produced a
skyscraper line that exhibits a wide-ranging picturesque
eclecticism, from effective streamlined nostalgia, as in the
Transco tower, to ambitious historical sendups, as in the
RepublicBank Center.

2

3

4

1. *PPG building, Pittsburgh. 1979–83.*
2. *RepublicBank Center, Houston, 1980–84.*
3. *580 California Street, San Francisco. 1983–84. Model.*
4. *Project for office building, Third Avenue at Fifty-Third Street, New York. 1980. Model.*

expensively executed details—tons of granite and pratfall playfulness notwithstanding. The entrance lobby is an oddly awkward and unsatisfactory space, distorted by its overreaching height and narrow dimensions. "Golden Boy," Evelyn Longman's huge statue of "The Spirit of Communication," moved from the outside of the old AT&T building, has been jacked up on a black base to canonical heights in the empty upper air. No amount of neck-craning achieves a dignified or workable perspective; the view is from the soles of the feet and the bottom of a well. Behind the statue's soaring plinth, the doors of "boutique" elevators solemnly open and shut. It is a very funny place in which all of the grand gestures have gone foolishly or fatuously awry, but one doubts that this was the kind of wit the architects intended.

The necessary metamorphosis of borrowed, mannerist parts into a convincing whole never takes place; even at this size the facade between pediment and arcade is dull and ordinary; this is a skyscraper that thuds rather than soars. The postmodernist historical references add up to a kind of architectural malapropism at drop-dead scale. In all-too-solid stone and steel, the building has even lost its original, antimodernist shock value. It has turned out to be ponderously pedestrian.

The possibilities of cut-and-paste are endless. The immediate, and lasting, impression of the cardboard-like silhouette of the RepublicBank's "Flemish Gothic"

top in Houston is that its tricky outline is an exasperatingly flat and lifeless zigzag against the sky. The Art Deco Transco tower, in the Post Oak neighborhood—which like most Houston neighborhoods is an invention rather than a place—is a better effort because it is based on a successful skyscraper prototype. The reason Transco works and RepublicBank does not can be attributed to Transco's reliance on a well-understood model rather than on Grimm's fairy tales. Its "modernistic" precedents established the use of vertical lines and massing for a "streamlined" style that was eminently suitable for the romantic, soaring concept of the tall building in the earlier part of this century—a formula effectively updated in Transco's clear and mirror-glass interpretation. A trompe l'oeil shaft by day, it becomes a distinctive pattern of light at night. This was a skyscraper style that related remarkably well to the facts of the case. Unfortunately, stone entrances or arches at the ground level of both the Transco and the far less successful San Francisco "Deco" building are failed gestures. Although these elements are meant to mediate between the tower and the street, they serve neither that purpose, nor any other, convincingly.

The developer who is the client for many of these structures, Gerald Hines of Houston, has found that rental response relates directly to a building's recognition factor on the skyline. Identity and novelty give a builder a different product and a competitive edge. The size, importance, and number of Hines's buildings in

American cities has done a great deal to establish this increasingly familiar, commercially successful formula. But what is being sold is rarely architecture; it is a gimmick with a designer label. It is becoming a standard joke that some of the most dramatic details that suggest climactic views and spaces house mechanical equipment—an architectural put-on of consummate cynicism.

Hines uses other architects—I. M. Pei, and Skidmore, Owings, and Merrill, for example—although these architects still produce basically modernist, if somewhat loosened-up, buildings. It is the trickier, postmodern buildings that get the attention that translates into tenants and profits. If this level of sponsorship has predictable and sometimes pedestrian results, it is hard to blame a developer for staying with a sure thing rather than pursuing riskier architectural challenges. Hines's espousal of excellence has been a Sputnik-like breakthrough in a business known for its dedicated quest for new lows for the construction bottom line. At the same time, he describes his commitment in a revealingly candid way. "We do not collect architecture. We use it," he says. The limits of this kind of architectural patronage are clear.

If postmodern eclecticism is the answer to modernism, the battle of the styles has a long way to go. Instead of cookie-cutter modern, we are getting cookie-jar monuments. All are eye-catching and mind-boggling

5. *Transco tower, Houston. 1981–83.*

buildings, and all raise serious architectural issues. Critical commentary, on the whole, has dealt with nothing more substantial than their silhouettes. The Johnson, Burgee work is clever costume design or scenography; one hesitates to call it architecture at all. More interesting is Johnson's aesthetic volatility; this early and ardent champion of the modernist revolution takes pride in having been among the first to defect. What he favors now is the kind of style that Le Corbusier ridiculed as "the feather on a woman's head" in *Vers Une Architecture,* the slim volume published in 1923 that became the rallying cry for a generation that hoped to change the world. If irony is what the postmodernists want, there is plenty of it around. Their stand-up architectural one-liners have much more to do with fashion and merchandising than with style, and it is surprising how quickly the joke, and the impact, wear thin.

We are, then, at a most curious and contradictory moment, when the need for change and the craving for the familiar are claiming equal time and attention. Art must inevitably change; it is a dynamic force that moves with history if it is not to stagnate and die. Our desire for identity with an art that has meaning for our own time, at a universal level or at the level of our personal lives, is an enduring concern. Familiarity is reassuring, and identity, real or spurious, has an obvious appeal over anonymity. As we reevaluate modernism it is natural and desirable to look at traditional models

again, to seek touchstones of the past and to rediscover their values. What is peculiar—and peculiar to this moment—is the attempt to hybridize past and present in an unprecedented way, an effort that takes tremendous amounts of sophisticated knowledge, creative courage, and professional skill if it is to succeed.

The easiest answer has been the one that takes the least effort—some kind of direct historical recall. For the tall building, the scaleless, impersonal shaft can be bridged by recognizable, traditional motifs at the top and the bottom and the addition of a few suggestive details to the no-man's-land of the commercial middle. This is the approach generally favored by developers and corporate clients. The truth is that it always was; the decorative screens, grilles, and colonnades of Edward Durell Stone were as widely acclaimed as, and not very different from, some of Philip Johnson's user-friendly history; Stone's buildings delighted a public weary of less-is-more a quarter-century ago.

The new building for E. F. Hutton in New York—a joint venture of CBS and Gerald D. Hines Interests, designed by Roche, Dinkeloo, and Associates—is among those structures that follow this popular route. The difference between this design and the original CBS building of 1966, when Kevin Roche was a top designer in Eero Saarinen's office, is instructive. The contrast is equally great with Roche's more recent and dazzling United Nations Plaza Hotel. In the new building, Roche abandons the U.N. Plaza's adventur-

The most popular route to the past, and the one with the most immediate and universal appeal, is some kind of nostalgic recall. Kevin Roche's work of the 1980s has turned fully postmodern in its uses of the past. But neo-mansard tops and giant pilasters serve to emphasize the massing of volumes that is still his chief preoccupation and greatest strength.

1. *60 Wall Street, New York, 1984. Drawing.*
2. *Building for E. F. Hutton, New York, 1983. Model.*

ous, reflective geometry for an arcaded base and a mansard top. That this denatured historicism should be the answer to a century of search for expressive skyscraper form has its perverse aspects.

If the new building is timidly neo-mansard, the old CBS was courageously neo-nothing. "Black Rock," as the original CBS building was called from the time of its completion, puzzled an audience unprepared for its departures from orthodox modernism. Critics were so intent on differentiating between the building's "true" and "false" piers that the somber, stone-clad structure was not seen for what it really was—an early manipulation of structural rationalism. This is a direction that Roche has continued to follow in a series of extraordinary monuments. The original CBS building's trompe-l'oeil facade, which appears open or closed depending on one's approach and angle of vision, created deliberate, dark ambiguities at a time when architecture was supposed to be rational and open.

Roche's work of the 1980s has turned fully postmodernist in its uses of the past, although his forms still emphasize the abstract massing of volumes that is his continuing preoccupation and strength. Certainly one of the most striking monuments of the decade must be the Roche, Dinkeloo blockbuster scheduled for construction at 60 Wall Street; it securely challenges Loos's famous Tribune tower column in its unconventional use of that eternal and indefatigable classical theme. What separates Loos's paradoxical

radicalism and Roche's rethinking of the matter, however, is the way Roche's reinterpreted classicism serves as a solidly dramatic framework for the evocation of architectural and cultural values through calculated visual messages that double as abstract architectonic devices. In some ways, this design is close to John Moser's 1894 search for the ideal skyscraper, in which he found himself "getting very cloce to the Classic," and ended by enclosing the building's shaft in top-to-bottom pilasters which he then "manfully" pierced with windows. There is no mistaking Roche's greater mastery of this curious form.

If CBS was puzzling in the sixties, and AT&T was shocking in the seventies when its pedimented model hit the skyline and the press, the novelty disappeared in a surprisingly short time. For a design to remain shocking, or disturbing (which is not necessarily bad—Ledoux's early-nineteenth-century buildings are still magnificently disturbing) there has to be more to it than meets the eye. When an unconventional appearance grows out of a painstaking and creative analysis of the uses and synthesis of the sources being explored, usually done experimentally and as part of a systematic and developing search for new solutions, a kind of work is produced that continues to stimulate reactions to the theories proposed and the way in which they are carried out. This stimulation, which can be troubling or pleasing with equal legitimacy, draws one into a deeper understanding of how appearance relates to all of the

1

factors of reference and utility of which a building's vocabulary is constructed. Such integration is not easy; it is the conclusive test of an architectural vision and the only real route to style.

But there are many routes to the past. One of the more unusual ways of bringing past and present together today avoids the quest for a spurious "compatibility" in favor of an obvious and purposeful juxtaposition of old and new forms that is usually deliberately unconventional and can be consciously jarring. This risky and provocative method has been chosen by the New York firm of Kohn, Pedersen, Fox, an office that grew rapidly in the 1970s and reached the front line of practice in the 1980s, in both the size of its operation and of its skyscraper commissions.

Kohn, Pedersen, Fox's use of historical references is anything but a nostalgic replication of the architectural past or an easy play to the sentimentally familiar. A freely reworked extrapolation of a mixture of historical details executed in traditional materials is combined in a calculatedly untraditional way with the most modern materials, technologies, and forms. Sheer glass towers spring from classically detailed masonry bases; Euclidean geometry is wrapped in Palladian references. The two "conflicting" vocabularies are played off against one another for extreme and often startling contrasts. The purpose, however, is not to shock but to devise radical new ways to address the problems of the un-

A more unusual route taken by the New York firm of Kohn, Pedersen, Fox puts past and present together in an unexpected and unconventional kind of architectural assemblage. Glass towers spring from masonry bases; Euclidean geometry is wrapped in Palladian references.

1. *333 Wacker Drive, Chicago, 1980–83.*

2

3

2. *Project for 125 East Fifty-Seventh Street, New York, 1983–84. Model.*
3. *Project for Park Centre, Calgary, Alberta, 1983. Model.*
4. *Project for Third National Bank, Nashville, 1982–83. Model.*
5. *Project for Federal Street, Boston, 1982–84. Model.*

4

5

precedented size, scale, and anonymity of twentieth-century commercial and institutional construction, and the loss of reference and relationship between people and places. They deal in contradiction and paradox; at the same time that these striking buildings disrupt context and shatter scale, they try to suggest the continuity of the urban context, and to address the humanistic and aesthetic dimensions of the city. The solutions run the danger of becoming grossly formularized, but more often they are assured exercises that reward programmatic analysis. The firm has set itself a large order, and on what level this architecture succeeds or fails can be seriously debated, as one can also debate the possibilities of achieving such aims in the service of an economic imperative that makes considerations of such factors an anachronism or irony. Some very able designers are demonstrating the possibilities of a difficult and challenging eclecticism that relies on more than the ability to leaf through architectural picture books.

As the partners' expertise in this kind of adaptive reuse of the past progresses, however, the seductions of historical exploration increase, and the enthusiasm for the possibilities can get out of hand. The controlled drama of William Pedersen's 333 Wacker Drive in Chicago, for example, is still unsurpassed by any of the later and fussier work. This 1980 design achieves a balance and completeness—an objective sought since the earliest skyscrapers—without literal reliance on the historical, tripartite division of base, shaft, and top.

6. *Project for office tower, Houston, 1981–82. Model.*

The building's tautly curved glass front echoes the line and color of the water on the river side and is reshaped on the other elevations to fit the context of the street. The base is marked by a sleek, bold use of symmetrical, stepped horizontal bands of gray granite and green marble, a Deco-inspired device that "grounds" the glass facade with convincing skill. The final transition from the impersonal to the personal scale is made by a pair of columns fronting the glass entrance. Risky changes in form and materials and stylistic references work well here; they deal with the basic problems of the tall building with a knowing hand and eye.

Partner Arthur May's design for the Third National Bank Building of Nashville reaches its greatest refinement in its final version. Three masonry stories introduce an intermediate scale between the base and the shaft, so that the stone-framed glass bays of grouped windows no longer rise abruptly from the ground-floor colonnade. A terminating pediment that originally peaked above a central section to tie two flanking shafts together unites all the parts of the building in a crowning gesture that both moderates its mass and refers back to an intricate adjustment of the parts. Beneath this surface complexity one senses the underlying structure on which these elaborate and intriguing themes are being played. The strength of any design is in direct proportion to the ability with which all these perceptual levels are fused in a functioning, architectonic whole.

Arthur May is also the firm's partner in charge of design for a Canadian project in Calgary, Alberta; if built, it will consist of two fifty-story towers flanking a fifteen-story hotel. A symmetrical plan joins three buildings around a formally landscaped and architecturally ornamented central court surrounded by a thirty-foot-high quasi-baroque oval colonnade. At ground level, the buildings refer to Calgary's older facades; at intermediate height the hotel claims kinship with 1950s office buildings; the twin glass towers rise futuristically from a transitional, partially enclosing, granite frame.

In downtown Boston, a proposal for a fifty-two-story office building by William Pedersen takes its cues from the city's vintage financial buildings. The scaling device of stone-framed glazing is used again, in a fugue of different sizes. The facade curves with the old, downtown street, and a segmental plaza borrows a characteristic Boston space. The difference between this building and Pedersen's earlier 333 Wacker Drive in Chicago is striking; the architect explains the later design's more traditional look as a response to the Boston setting, but it coincides with the development of more involved stylistic investigations. The building, startling to some and reassuring to others, is carried out in a convincing and thoroughly unacademic classicism. It recalls Parisian Beaux Arts and Roman neoclassicism of the early twentieth century, when most academically trained practitioners were very uncomfortable with the tall building. Pedersen is obviously completely at ease. The fact that this "new classicism" suggests a long tradition through familiar references plays a considerable part in the public acceptance of structures that are not nearly as simple or familiar as they seem. Perhaps the modernist interregnum was necessary before older vocabularies could be carried so confidently into a new context; these designs put the accent on both parts of the word postmodernism, for an ambitious stylistic synthesis.

There is a return to the highly disciplined drama of Pedersen's Wacker Drive building in Chicago in his proposal for an enormous Houston skyscraper, a building that makes a strong statement about the radical separation of its parts. A curved four-story section at the base offers a gesture to the domestic scale of nearby houses; this element fronts the soaring, curved glass shaft that rises precipitously behind it; the frontal curve becomes a series of sharp, shallow glass angles at the side. An intermediate, stone-faced shaft has a grid pattern of square windows. The design rests its case on an extraordinary series of unorthodox relationships meant to fragment the huge mass visually, and to reduce its impact at ground level. This is an architecture closer to Houdini than to Alberti.

The technique here is one of assemblage rather than of adaptation; older stylistic conventions take on new meanings in their wholly different use and context. As William Pedersen explained in the text of the firm's entry in the Southwest BankShares competition in Houston, "Elements of nostalgia and contemporary culture, both retrospective and prophetic, have been fused into a single piece." Sullivan's theme that a skyscraper must be a single thing survives; the measure of wholeness continues to apply. But as the projects get larger and more daring, the ostensible purpose of their underlying philosophy—a mitigating effect on scale and context—becomes impossible to realize. Such tour-de-force towers—one is proposed as a replacement for an urbane Fifth Avenue block in New York—would destroy the intimacy, variety, and quality of fine small buildings for bruising bulk and a bag of dazzling tricks.

Another architect who is pushing the frontiers of eclecticism hard is Helmut Jahn, of the Chicago firm of Murphy, Jahn. From the bold exploitation of building technology—which he does with sleight-of-hand skill—he has gone on to an increasing interest in abstract solutions. Jahn uses radical engineering for remarkable images with extravagant ease. Image, in fact, is primary in Jahn's work, but the impact of these images rests on two things: his manipulation of structure and technology and his broad borrowings of evocative design details. Not the least is his remarkable flair for architectural theatrics.

In Jahn's 1978–82 addition to the Chicago Board of Trade, he pays homage to the original Board of Trade building designed and constructed by Holabird

2

Helmut Jahn of Murphy, Jahn is pushing the frontiers of expressionism exceptionally hard. His inventive energy has moved from the exploitation of technology to a creative eclecticism that yields a space-age synthesis of past and future.

1.   Chicago Board of Trade building, completed by Holabird and Root in 1930. Drawing.
2.   Addition to Chicago Board of Trade by Murphy, Jahn, 1978–82. Drawing.

1

3

4

3. *1 South Wacker, Chicago, 1980–81.*
4. *701 Fourth Avenue South, Minneapolis, 1982–84.*
5. *11 Diagonal Street, Johannesburg, South Africa, 1981–84. Model.*
6. *Project for Wilshire-Midvale tower, Los Angeles, 1983. Model.*

5

6

and Root (the firm name changed from Holabird and Roche in 1928) in the late 1920s and early 1930s. But he seems to be influenced by the beautiful, fifty-year-old presentation drawing of the early building as much as by the building itself; the rendering's handsome highlights and smoky shadows clearly delight him. Jahn's own drawing of the new and old buildings, done half a century later, is equally remarkable; it carries the romantic 1930s image to an extravagant space-age poetry.

All of Jahn's drawings are notably spectacular; they stand out even at a moment when architectural drawings are enjoying renewed popularity and appeal. His tall buildings rise from a setting of sunstruck or twilit towers that seem to be borne aloft by layers of beacons exploding from their setbacks and spires. There is no more effective dramatization of the idealized glory of the tall building than Jahn's reinterpretation of the glamorous visions and innocent aspirations of the past. This is the apotheosis of the skyscraper. That same vision was first expressed in Hugh Ferriss's soft, shadowed charcoal renderings of abstract skyscraper forms, just after World War I. Technically, they were meant to illustrate the possibilities of the "zoning envelope" established by New York's new zoning law of 1916; in spirit, they were closer to the prismatic expressionism of Bruno Taut's monumental fantasies of 1919, in which he confidently reshaped the Alps into crystalline structures—an Olympian precursor of environmental art. Reality is finally catching up with Ferriss's evocative forms today.

The post–World War I skyscraper emphasized technology and profits; modernist pragmatism renounced the tall building as theater. Today, postmodernist architects portray their towers with flash and fantasy; in construction, these buildings combine cultural and technological references that would have been impossible a short time ago. Jahn's more far-out designs —and one wonders how long they will seem that extreme—tend to display a sometimes alarming panache. Buildings such as his Wilshire-Midvale tower for Los Angeles and an office project for New York's Lexington Avenue that feature spreading tops and shiny skins in stripes and plaids are extreme excursions into expressive surface qualities—a kind of zoot-suit architecture. They seek their sources in almost unlimited design options; they do not confine themselves to playing hopscotch with history.

There is apparently no end to the variety of the products of Jahn's inventive mind. But questions have been raised about his work; the architectural writer Nory Miller, reporting on Chicago's "Babel of New Towers" in the April 1984 issue of *Chicago* magazine, characterized some of these scintillating concepts as "reasonable ideas and genuine talent foundering from shortfalls of technique." The substantial sense of quality perfected by the practitioners of the High Modern Corporate style has not yet been achieved in these novel towers. "Close up they seem like tinsel," she wrote; "their detail is considerably more charming at tabletop scale."

Jahn can probably be charged with pushing aesthetic license to its limits, but that is the mood of the moment, and he is not alone. Designs like the intriguing giant juke box for the Northwestern Terminal building in Chicago can be far more interesting than outrageous if he masters technique as well as effect. The Diagonal Street skyscraper in Johannesburg, South Africa, reaches a literal pinnacle of image-architecture, while his prizewinning design for the Southwest Center in Houston bases its soaring, faceted form on an innovative use of structural steel. But no matter what degree of picturesque drama is pursued, both concepts owe a clear debt to advances in engineering.

Jahn's expressed intent is to go beyond the established horizons of history and technology. Like William Pedersen, he too has explained his design philosophy in the text that accompanied his entry in the Houston Southwest tower competition. "Our involvement with the skyscraper has to be seen in an historical framework," he wrote. "We look to the immediate past—which is now a tradition—and to the remote past for inspiration. . . . We believe the Modern Movement is not dead and its principles can be extended and continued. . . ." Jahn's not exactly underreaching purpose is to find a "strategy [that] can generate totally new and striking images and extend the limits of architecture.

. . . Our interest is in form, image and expression which encompass yet transcend technological determinants." He has reaffirmed the need for poetic license: "Architecture cannot be solely a rational process."

Neomodernism

Another aspect of postmodernism is far less of a break with modernism than a calculated extension of it—a trend that might be called neomodernism. Like neoclassicism, it reworks an established vocabulary. These buildings emphasize an artful, geometrical abstraction based on the aesthetic formulas and specific details of early modernism: such details are handled with both sentiment and rigor. What is most significant is the way the practitioners of this architecture have moved it far beyond early modernism in the definition and creation of space. The complex uses of transparency and reflection, an increasing ambiguity of closed and open elements, a layering of spaces operating on many levels at once, enlarge the range of visual and sensory experiences. There is a precise and subtle new formalism here as well, in which early-modernist details are savored for their own sake; ramps, rails, and cantilevers are celebrated as formal aesthetic devices.

This is a conceptual and physical breakthrough with enormous aesthetic consequences for the art of architecture. In the work of Richard Meier, for example, circulation patterns are the ordering element for the exploration of kinetic effects and perceptual possibilities. The firm of Gwathmey, Siegel translates the suave streamlining of the 1930s into a hard-edged, worldly elegance executed in pastel postmodern hues. The most individualistic interpretations have appeared in the strikingly virtuosic work of the Japanese architect Arata Isozaki, who has moved on to even more complex and provocative designs increasingly infused with history, metaphor, and kitsch. But there is nothing stale or tired about this kind of modernist recall; it possesses an extraordinary creative vitality. The new interpretation of existing conventions leads to a distinctly new art form.

Interestingly enough, this development is less a continuous and natural evolution of modernism than a conscious revival by a younger generation; these architects look back at the pioneering International Style of the early twentieth century as a historical phenomenon rather than as the true believer's path to aesthetic salvation. They see its vintage components as a set of appealing forms and symbols that intrigue them far more than the messages those forms were originally meant to convey.

Perhaps what is of more significance for architecture today is the fact that virtually everything is seen as history now—even that most recent event of the historical past, the modern movement. Distance has lent not only enchantment but a totally changed vision and point of view. Until recently, the architecture of the twentieth century was conceived as something that existed only in, and of, the present, for the future. The new attitude turns its back on the present, and even on the immediate past, as if that aberrant revolution called modernism had never occurred. It is this abrupt change of position that is the most important, and radical, aspect of current philosophy and practice.

The fallacy of this attitude, however, is the belief that something new can be created by rejecting those conditions and contributions that are necessary for the transformation of any art form. An even more basic fallacy is the idea that those elements can be rejected by choice, or at all. There is absolutely no way to purge today's building of the revolutions in thought, design, and technology that are intrinsic to the modern movement; they are embedded in the way buildings are constructed and used for contemporary life. Denouncing them will not remove them from either history or reality. Revivals of older urban or architectural models can instruct and sensitize. But the most impressive and valid developments in the architecture of the present moment are those that build on the unique achievements of the twentieth century rather than attempt to deny them; the best work is that which carries the legacy of modernism to revealing and greatly enriched new dimensions. References to the past, or the incorporation of a more permissive architectural vocabulary, make the challenge, and the potential, greater.

There are hazards involved; the pursuit of what is essentially a formal approach can lead to some exquisite dead ends. The theoretical projects of Peter Eisenman, for example, have the immutable elegance of mathematical equations whose intractable perfection is highly resistant to the realities of living. The question is whether this kind of work can be anything more than an abstraction; when built, the inconveniences to the inhabitants are as serious as the architect's intentions. The danger is the suggestion that brilliant architectural exercises are enough, that they need no sullying entanglements with the real world. There is an endless enchantment with cerebral calculations and the sound of symbols clashing.

On the other hand, the formal fantasies of an architect like John Hejduk are pure poetic license, combining literary and aesthetic references in a unique series of lyrical images, often in the form of haunting narrative subjects full of mystery and metaphor. Such exercises as ''The Cemetery for the Ashes of Thought,'' or ''The Thirteen Towers of Canareggio'' can be so extraordinarily moving and so seductive that their execution is beside the point. Eisenman's work is conceptually at the opposite pole from Hejduk's, but both are devoted to exploring the limits of architectural imagery and response. We do not live by buildings alone.

Neomodernism and other work conceived in the modernist tradition have produced some of the more impressive tall buildings of the 1980s. Cesar Pelli's glass-walled skyscrapers carry Mies's transparent towers to a more highly developed version of that consummate twentieth-century glass aesthetic. Unlike those who consider the curtain wall no more than the plain or fancy wrapper of packaged commercial space, Pelli sees it as a vehicle for expressive architectural detailing. Design solutions are better, he believes, when they are consistent with the way something is actually built, and those ideas and practices that are common to a time provide the best opportunities for art.

Pelli consistently proves his case by designing some extraordinarily sensitive skyscraper skins. If he cannot make excessive size or bulk acceptable, he tries to ameliorate it by turning oversized towers into objects of precisely analyzed, remarkable refinement. His is a well-mannered artistry. He does not seek bombast; he divides, frames, and color-codes the thin, light, vitreous wall that is part of the modern technological miracle of skyscraper engineering, treating it as a taut, enveloping membrane or as a smooth aggregate of discreetly designed panels and subtly graded parts. As he moves farther away from "pure" modernism, he wraps his skins around the building in layers of glass and stone, like jackets, for an increasingly formal symmetry and sculptural form. The towers of New York's Battery Park City commercial core—which will be the city's most monumental building group—have skins that are a graduated mix of masonry and mirror-glass, growing glassier as they rise to their geometric caps; the greater use of stone facing at the lower levels is meant to recall and relate to existing Manhattan street scale and detail.

Pelli's work could be Sullivan "up-to-date," as Montgomery Schuyler would have put it. Schuyler would probably have been pleased by the finesse of these intricate, reflective expressions of use and context. Since the 1960s, Pelli has responded thoughtfully and without excess to liberated architectural attitudes. But his precise and subtle art is still close to "the thing itself." In none of this work is structure divorced from style; there are none of the conscious atectonic heresies with which the postmodernists outrage the modernists. Structure is treated both as a generator of architectural form and as a source of architecturally self-sustaining elements to be explored, in turn, for their own formalist aesthetic. A meticulous and consistent relationship is maintained to a basic architectonic rationale.

The work of the London firm of Foster Associates is a particularly striking example of the continuing use of a strong structural aesthetic—but with a significant postmodernist difference. Norman Foster is fascinated by the possibilities of technology as an art form and symbol rather than as a purely physical means to an aesthetic end. Technology, in fact, is his particular expressive tool. While the visual magic of the sheer, illusory glass wall of the Willis Faber building in Ipswich is a product of modern glass manufacture and methods of joinery, it is as a marvelous play on reflection and dematerialization that it makes its architectural statement. In the Sainsbury Center for the Arts, the drama of the huge truss is celebrated above all. The

Cesar Pelli's glass-skinned skyscrapers carry Mies's glass-tower precedent to a more complex version with an aesthetic rationale tied to both modern building technology and the buildings' context.

1

3

1. *Museum of Modern Art tower, New York, 1977–84.*
2. *Battery Park City commercial center, New York, 1980.*
Model.
3. *Norwest Center, Minneapolis, 1984. Model.*

2

skyscraper headquarters for the Hong Kong and Shang-hai Banking Corporation in Hong Kong, an enor-mously complex and expensive structure, is defined theatrically by the immense, truss-braced walls. Foster buildings stress machine precision for the most polished and powerful effect. This is engineering for art's sake; the limited, and limiting, definitions of modernism's relationship to technology have been totally exploded. The firm's entry in the competition to design a new headquarters for Humana, Inc., in Louisville seems more suitable for outer space than for middle America. The thought of Foster's antenna-topped Darth Vader tower on a Louisville streetcorner must have staggered Humana's corporate imagination; it did not win. But there is no denying the ingenuity and beauty of many of these structures; again, characteristically, they have been pushed to the limits of expression.

Although the current multiplicity of routes to a more expressive architecture is being called a pluralistic phenomenon, it is so only in a superficial sense. In all of the variety of approach, there is less of a real diversity of styles than a diversity of means to the same end. No matter how dissimilar the source or the inspiration, all of the design elements employed are removed from their original context and purpose to exist on their own as discrete, independent forms, or as pure stylistic devices. This is true whether these elements are classical columns or industrial components. And it is this over-riding fact that unites and characterizes as a single

The work of Foster Associates stresses the expressive drama of structure; technology is Norman Foster's most important tool. The visible trusses of the Hong Kong and Shanghai Banking Corporation building in Hong Kong, designed in 1980, theatrically define the engineering emphasis. Model photomontage.

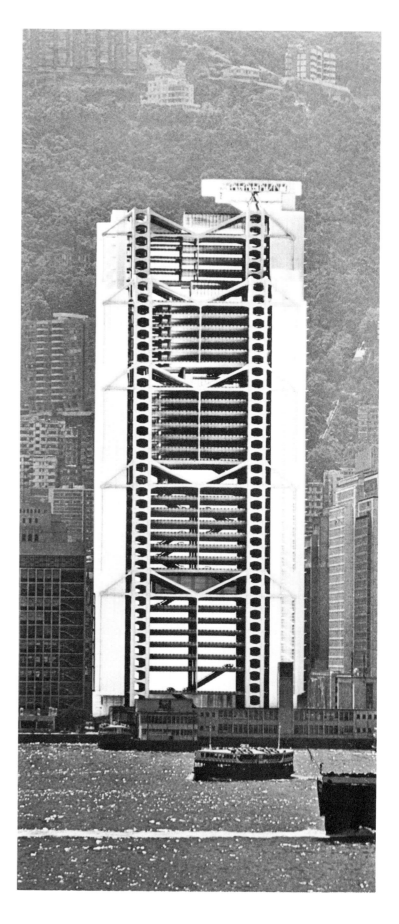

aesthetic product the work of those engaged in today's stridently competitive dialectics, no matter how much they may divide and protest.

The State of the Skyscraper Art

It is clear that everyone is playing the game of "Can You Top This?" very seriously, and for very high stakes. One significant side effect has been the re-emergence of the design competition, fifty years after the Chicago Tribune tower competition made sky-scraper history. The circumstances are remarkably similar: the art of architecture is again in radical transition, and the skyscraper, as an art form, is experiencing enormous visibility. Like the results of the Tribune tower competition, today's entries represent the full and fascinating range of current theory and practice; they dramatically summarize the state of the art of the tall building in the 1980s.

In 1982, a limited, invited competition for a new headquarters building for Humana, Inc., a hospital-management company based in Louisville, created a remarkable parallel to the earlier event. The program carried a direct reference to the example of the Tribune tower and expressed Humana's wish for a singular skyscraper of notable artistic quality. In contrast to the Tribune tower's open contest, which drew hundreds of entries from all over the world, Humana's was limited to five firms. But those five designs offer a textbook presentation of today's leading trends. The range is startling, from the postmodern classicism of Michael Graves's winning design with its loggia, balcony, pilasters, and earth-tone polychromy, to the futuristic technology of Foster Associates' trussed-tube, antenna-topped circular tower. Between these schemes is the self-described "audacity" of Murphy, Jahn's ascending spiral of giant metallic trusses and glittering glass, in which technology becomes a dazzling display of pattern and decoration as much as a demonstration of the marvels of engineering. The entry by Cesar Pelli and Associates is a symmetrical, prismatic octagon with a tapered stainless-steel crown; the building is progressively layered with lighter and more reflective granite and glass skins that change from a warm red-brown to cool silver. Pelli moves modernism into expressionism with a sense of restraint. A formal design by Ulrich Franzen, K. Kroeger, and Associates is a thoughtful but rather dry compromise between tradition and modernism.

What ties these seemingly irreconcilable approaches together is the fact that each design employs its forms and techniques symbolically; the power of the image created is of primary importance, and the chosen vocabulary is used to that end. Graves's prizewinning building, on which construction began immediately, seems far less overtly referential and relentlessly picturesque in its final version than some of his smaller, earlier projects. His original sketches of skyscraper-keeps and temple-dungeons, more suggestive of Rapunzel's tower

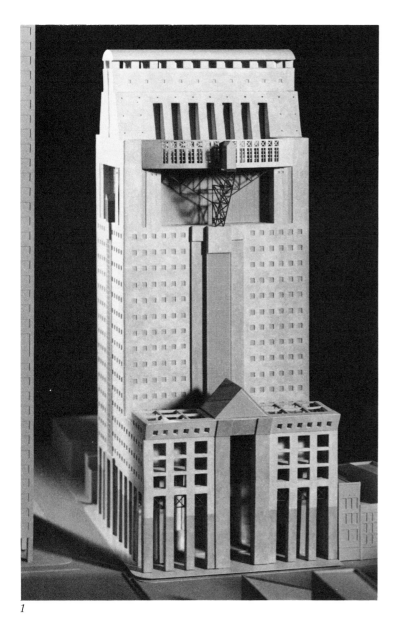

1

2

3

4

Six decades after the landmark competition for the Chicago Tribune tower, the search for a skyscraper style stands at a similar threshold of creative change. Now, as then, skyscraper competitions most tellingly reveal the current state of the art. In 1982, five invited designs for the Humana, Inc., headquarters in Louisville offered significant and remarkable variety. The winning submission by Michael Graves, in which modernism is totally abandoned for a fully committed romantic classicism, was chosen over the more conservative eclecticism of Ulrich Franzen and Cesar Pelli and the flamboyant high tech of Norman Foster and Helmut Jahn.

1. *Michael Graves, Architects.*
2. *Foster Associates.*
3. *Ulrich Franzen, K. Kroeger and Associates.*
4. *Cesar Pelli and Associates.*

5

than of the modern city, became a much more ordered and urbanistic design in the actual building.

There is an interesting comparison to be made between Graves's story-book approach in these preliminary sketches and one of Louis Sullivan's handkerchief-sized preliminary pencil drawings for a midwestern bank. In the tiny Sullivan sketch, every aspect of the building's structure and style, even to the location and feathery details of the ornament, are already present in a miracle of conceptualization and delineation. Even in miniature, the Sullivan building is fully architectonic from the start. In Graves's drawings, one senses pictorial rather than structural priorities.

Most of the Humana entries were accompanied by seductive texts that make persuasive cases for designs and philosophies that are light years—and styles—apart and which, by any logic, should be mutually unjustifiable. Some architects are considerably more articulate than others. Graves's written rationale devotes a good deal of space to attacking modernism—a cause as popular as motherhood with a public long confused and turned off by austere and unfamiliar forms. The case for his building rests to a large degree on that rejection. Whether the actual and metaphysical messages about the uses of the past succeed will be clear only when the building has taken its place in the city. A sympathetic corporate client has made the kind of materials available that had to be sacrificed to economy in Graves's earlier Portland, Oregon, Public Office building.

There is still another parallel between the Tribune and Humana competitions. The winning designs in both rely on the use of a traditional vocabulary, with an obvious appeal for the client. Howells and Hood's Chicago tower enhances its superbly articulated shaft with highly skilled Gothic detail that gives immediate, evocative pleasure to the eye. Graves's design also appeals strongly for its suggestive historicism. The difference between the two is both subtle and significant: Howells and Hood's solution followed the accepted academic rules of its time, while Graves's building, in spite of its traditional elements, is anything but academic; its uses of the past are far more radical than its appearance implies.

This "classical eclecticism" is, in fact, the most radical of the current new directions in skyscraper architecture, not because it espouses the classical sources that the modernists so emphatically rejected, but because it is the first skyscraper style to consciously flout "the facts of the case," to reject the continuing imperative of structure as a chief generator of architectural style. There is no longer the assumption that an architectural aesthetic should express, reinforce, refer to, or take its cues from the physical and structural realities of the building. This is a total departure from the virtually unbroken line of structural determinism that has been a basic tenet of skyscraper design.

The widely varied historical guises of the Tribune tower entries dealt with "the thing itself." Graves's themes and details deliberately mask, or suppress, or even deny "the facts of the case"; they have ceased to be important, or relevant, in the architect's mind. The relationship of structure and style that has been at the heart of the skyscraper aesthetic since its beginning has been significantly and deliberately ruptured. Buildings like this are sending unfamiliar signals and messages. Post and beam, column and pediment, are no longer to be understood as the expressive elements of traditional structural systems; since these systems have been supplanted, and the efforts to express the new systems have been judged a failure by postmodernist critics, the traditional architectural elements are revived to serve as signs and metaphors for the secure and established values of the past.

What is not commonly realized, in the general delight at having something recognizable to respond to again, is that this departure is a far more unconventional and controversial kind of design than the most futuristic space-age towers sporting lasers and heliports and claiming to be "instruments of communication." Such are the ironies of perception and taste, and of architecture today.

Another limited competition was held in 1982 by the Southwest BancShares Corporation and the Century Development Company of Houston. The program called for a landmark skyscraper, a hundred-story building, give or take a dome or a spire, for the exact center of downtown Houston. (Southwest BancShares subsequently merged with the Mercantile Texas Corporation to become the Mercantile Southwest Organization; the building, called Southwest Center, will presumably be big enough for all.) Because the site is small, the tower takes the form of an enormously tall and slender shaft.

Again, the sponsors invoked the Tribune tower competition to ask for a "major contribution to urban architecture," a structure of "timeless institutional" and "distinctive architectural" character that would be a "prominent architectural profile on the Houston skyline." The program called for the now-customary observation deck and restaurant at the top, a requirement conspicuously compatible with the design of the newest skyscrapers, which are considered incomplete without party hats, regal crowns, or ambitious "fioratura." (Ah, the top! The game is being played most strenuously and inventively at the top.)

After interviews, the field was narrowed to ten firms, of which three—Kohn, Pedersen, Fox of New York; Skidmore, Owings, and Merrill of Houston; and Murphy, Jahn of Chicago—reached the final stage. The winning design, by Helmut Jahn, is a tower of great theatrical presence and romantic appeal, its eighty-two stepped and tapered, needle-topped stories soaring to a height of 1,400 feet—FAA willing. The building breaks the Federal Aviation Administration's height limitations in the Houston area.

1

Another competition, for Southwest BancShares of Houston in 1982, called for "the tallest building west of the Mississippi" and also drew conscious parallels with the Chicago Tribune tower. The winning design was by Murphy, Jahn, with two runners-up—by Kohn, Pedersen, Fox and by Skidmore, Owings, and Merrill.

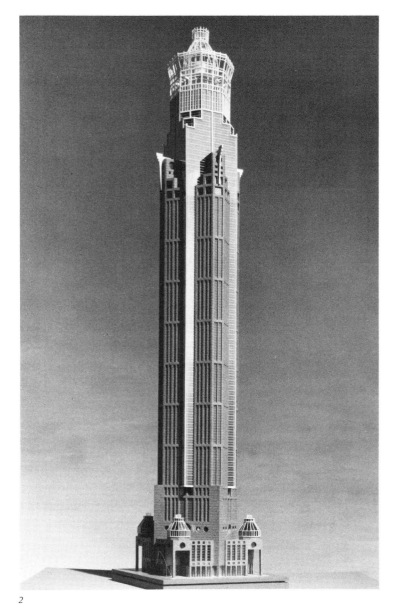

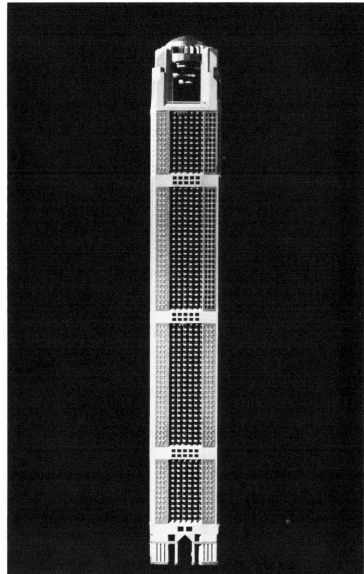

1. Murphy, Jahn.
2. Kohn, Pedersen, Fox.
3. Skidmore, Owings, and Merrill.

The creative range of the three designs is remarkable, and the presentation drawings and models are quite breathtakingly beautiful. A great deal of thought has been given to the basic problems of the tall building's scale, symbolism, orientation, and setting, and to the way it meets the street and the sky. The architects have waxed particularly eloquent in their written presentations; not the least interesting parts of these competitions are the statements that describe philosophy and methodology. They form a revealing manifesto of the new architecture.

The firm of Skidmore, Owings, and Merrill, the most consistent and enduring producer of the High Modern skyscraper, held closest to the modernist structural-aesthetic rationale for a building with one foot in the postmodernist camp. The design, by Richard Keating of the Houston office, which looks like an enormous bell tower with a column-clasped glass dome reminiscent of Bernard Maybeck and the San Francisco Exposition style or a hybrid of Mission and Beaux Arts, is essentially derived from its unusual engineering; structure has always been a strong point at SOM. It is described in terms of the structural performance of corner columns, rigid zones and aerolastic damping (the interaction of the building with the pressure of the wind) in much dull prose and dogged detail. Except for one reference to "the crystalline dome held on four sides like a diamond solitaire," there are no flights of fancy.

William Pedersen's dissertation for the Kohn, Pedersen, Fox entry, on the other hand, is a rather heady dose of history and theory that indulges in a far more cosmic rationale. He refers to the firm's design as "subjective and fanciful . . . carrying associations of past, present and future." It is he who describes the octagonal, openwork crown of the building as "fioratura." That's a hard one to top. Although it takes some imagination to see this structure as an extension of Houston's "genius loci"—whatever that may symbolize beyond the maximization of the value of downtown land—it is a striking, if somewhat confectionary design combining structure and spun sugar. The facts of the case are there in fancy dress.

Helmut Jahn's winning design is even more fanciful, but like the Skidmore, Owings, and Merrill entry, it is explained in terms of its unusual technology. This faceted shaft is no arbitrary exercise in origami; it grows out of innovative and sophisticated engineering based on two sets of interior diagonal braces that straddle the core and transfer the loads to massive concrete columns. "The structural rationale for such a tall structure is technically and economically inescapable," Jahn writes in the presentation text. The small base and extreme height dictated the need for structural ingenuity in all of the solutions, but for Jahn, obviously, engineering is only the beginning. With characteristic panache, he uses advanced technology to create a sense of nostalgia for the "futuristic" past.

The sponsors now have a stunning proposal, ambitions to match, and two turndowns from the FAA (the original refusal was appealed and a reversal denied in January, 1984). Unlike most cities, Houston has no zoning controls, and since Federal height limitations are advisory, this leaves the final decision up to the builder. With the project in limbo, the developers were, at last word, busy renting the still-unbuilt offices and wrestling with their souls and the FAA.

Beyond the Facades

Judgment of the new buildings, in terms of use, aesthetics, and environment, can be made only on completion and in context. They take enormous, conscious risks. The new freedom has created unparalleled opportunities and a time of dramatic promise and challenge. The bottom line is the critical question: What kind of architecture is being produced? Unfortunately, there seems to be little interest in answering it. Either out of genuine enthusiasm or a need to be with, and of, the new in art, few commentators are analyzing or evaluating the results with much critical objectivity. This, also, is not new; the role of club member or camp follower has always been more attractive than being considered out of it or incapable of understanding the new vision and values. And as has happened with so much of the art of our time, architectural criticism is becoming a game in itself, with an increasingly inaccessible language and a growing detachment from the built object. The buildings can hardly be seen for the words. Publicity is more important than the product.

The modernists, in their own day, were equal offenders, of course, although the language employed was usually more righteous than silly or smart. A great deal of uninspired, extremely ordinary, and very bad building was praised or excused by those who professed to be critics because it followed the right—or the fashionable—rules. Apologists operated in the guise of analysts, and still do. Lessons that should have been learned early by astute observers were glossed over or ignored. This has finally caused the delayed backlash to modernism that is unfortunately sweeping good and bad into the same discard heap. And the same kind of over-publicized underachievement is being touted as trend-setting today.

It is hard not to see some of the most aggressively promoted examples of postmodernism, hailed as architectural breakthroughs, as surprisingly thin and inconsequential buildings. A do-it-yourself, kit-of-parts eclecticism turns the promise of revived grandeur into a paper-dollhouse architecture of plastic and plywood pilasters, and pediments, and sheet-rock cut-outs. There is too much that is too cute, pretending to be erudite or clever. Personal stylistic statements are preferred to optimum solutions.

The conflict between function and expression is not new either; this is a legitimate, historic condition of architecture, and the manner in which the necessary equilibrium is achieved is intrinsic to the quality of the result. But the trade-off today is increasingly unbalanced, and the "architectural celebration of the mixed metaphor," as the critic John Pastier has put it, is a distinctly mixed bag. "Although its aims of richness, esthetic freedom, symbolic meaning and historic reference are all laudable in the abstract," Pastier has written, "the concrete products of the post-modernist sensibility tend to be caricatures of old architecture or disingenuously superficial essays." The most generous evaluation of much of this work is to call it transitional, hoping that it will go where it is headed quickly. It is hard to take these architects as seriously as they take themselves.

What is significant, and disturbing, is the fact that the most questionable hallmarks of this particular kind of building are characteristic of much culture and the process that passes for education today. A narrow, narcissistic intelligence and sensibility, even among the exceptionally gifted, seeks easy effects and instant gratification in the naïve belief that shattering discoveries are being made. There is an exaggerated sense of uniqueness and an adolescent wit. Unexceptional personal preoccupations are offered as epochal creative advances; shallow observations are touted as profound, and small ironies are passed off as cosmic wisdom. This seems to be the intellectual distemper of our times.

But architecture is not trivia, and it is more than skin-deep. To give appropriate form to structure, plan, purpose, and place, and to do so with dignity and expressive content, is a good deal more than the fulfillment of a passing fancy. The art of building is the difficult act of design that turns physical needs and realities into an aesthetic experience of personal and universal value. The success or failure of a building is measurable by these constant factors that operate within any style, and that transcend it.

The special considerations that control the design of the skyscraper have been investigated in a recently completed five-volume monograph called *The Planning and Design of Tall Buildings,* published by the Council on Tall Buildings and Urban Habitat of the American Society of Civil Engineers. This ambitious study deals with everything from philosophy to engineering stability. Inevitably the technology of the skyscraper is the most evident of these special features; height is primarily a function of technology. The engineering development of the tall building is one of the truly remarkable chapters in the history of architecture, and it has been well documented in the standard texts. Structure is what the tall building is about, even if this seems like belaboring the obvious; as its basic fact and most critical element, it is structure that is at the heart of the tall building's design. It becomes the architect's most powerful expressive tool, by the very nature of the constructive art.

But structural innovation and aesthetic preference can expand choices only as long as the real estate and investment numbers work out. Today's large commercial structures, like those that came before them, are essentially an economic formula. The modern office building has been standardized as a central service core surrounded by 15,000 to 25,000 square feet of space, or multiples of those figures. This standard has been set by business itself as the optimum working floor area for the large corporation. The tower shape is also dictated by the investor's belief that ground floor retail space is best concentrated for the largest possible captive working population that can be channeled through it each day. Even the tall building's almost uniform four- or five-foot design module has evolved out of another economic consideration, the minimum office size for standardized corporate needs.

Since almost anything is possible technologically today—the architect designs and the engineer makes it stand up—even the basic structure is subject to economic determination. It is hideously expensive to build high. Within the market calculations the modern skyscraper is squeezed into the mold made by zoning laws and building codes. Ultimately, the design of the tall building is a product of investment economics and urban politics.

But there are other, less pragmatic factors that influence the decision to build tall, of which much is usually made. The desire to convey image, status, power, and prestige, to signal economic or cultural dominance, is universally acknowledged. Not least—although it is seldom discussed in the corridors of corporate or political power—is the architect's desire to create a museum-worthy object, usually against considerable odds; it is the artist's ego-play against the builder's. The drive for immortality, or at least for the accolades of the art establishment, is always present. There is, finally, in the words of the Council on Tall Buildings, the basic human desire "to build to the very limits of strength and knowledge . . . to achieve the limits of the achievable." This is the ultimate, eternal, and irresistible challenge.

The catalyst and unifying force for all of these conflicting concerns has been the search for style. The enormous rational and romantic diversity of skyscraper design makes this increasingly clear. It has not been the race for height that architects have cared about nearly as much as finding suitable and memorable ways to enclose the structure that makes that height possible. In an article that appeared almost forty years ago in *Architectural Forum,* the editors made the telling observation that the structural principles of the tall building, developed by the turn of the century, have remained essentially unchanged. That fact, they noted with acerbic disapproval, "throws into harsh relief the vacillations of the facades."

Ah, those vacillating facades, shivering in the hard, cold light of structural reason and editorial censure. But if we look at those vacillations without prejudice or prejudgment, they tell us more about architecture than

The structural principles of the tall building, well developed by the turn of the century, have remained essentially unchanged. What do change are the ways in which the building systems are enclosed or expressed. For those who believe that form follows function, these changes are a sign of a lack of commitment to structural logic; in the words of Architectural Forum almost fifty years ago, they "throw into harsh relief the vacillation of the facades." For historians, they reveal the challenges and uncertainties of tall-building design and the state of the art at any given moment. They are the evidence of the continuing, creative search for a skyscraper style.

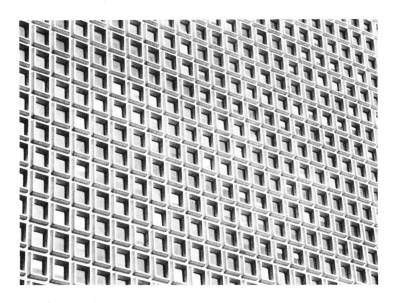

many people really want to know, or the experts find acceptable. The variety of those facades gives the lie to ideologues, who like their style straight, conforming neatly to the party line. The variety makes pluralism a fact, not just a passing fancy. The facades separate the artists from the hacks, the radicals from the conservatives, and the poets from the hired guns. They show us that the history of the skyscraper, which is also the history of this century—and which is like so much of that history—is a search for identity.

In the end, however, a building is only as good as its resolution of the complex structural, social, and symbolic factors involved. Style is the result of the architect's most concentrated and comprehensive efforts to resolve those often irreconcilable factors in an expressive synthesis at the level of art. But he has never had an easy job or a clearly defined role in dealing with the tall building. The choice has been between two conflicting courses. He could either proclaim his power, and his right, to turn the engineer's and the economist's calculations into an art form that carries the special freight of responsiveness to people and the environment, or he could disclaim any power to do anything about these controlling factors at all.

Most architects have opted for the first course; those who simply settled for being the developer's drafting arm have traditionally been scorned. But today attitudes toward skyscraper design are changing in a way that is profoundly disturbing. It has become fashionable for the architect to profess that he is unable to affect the basic building package. Many postmodernists prefer to consider the skyscraper just that—an enormous package that can be decorated for status, symbolism and style. This is done, as a rule, through a hierarchy of historical symbols, an élite checklist of aesthetic references. Released from any other concerns about the behemoth he is designing, the architect plays to the press and his peers. He is free to be erudite, nostalgic, or droll, and, if he can carry it off, fashionably outrageous. The layman may not always recognize the source, but it is clear that the architect is a very clever fellow. Whether this attitude toward design is a breakthrough or an abdication is open to serious debate. But to say that the skyscraper is no more than a package of standardized space to be gift-wrapped to the architect's or the client's taste is to make architecture less than an art or a profession.

The Skyline and the City

There are some who believe that the skyscraper has reached the end of the line; that it has become too large, too frivolous, too destructive of people or places. Although it remains the most stunning architectural challenge of our time, one can no longer escape or deny the fact that the newest towers, larger and more impressive and more overreaching than ever, are just as stunning exercises in the violation of cities. One cannot turn one's back on the fact that the skyscraper is being so patently

Whatever the design, however, the tall building is a product of investment economics and urban politics. Whatever the trends in taste, it is ultimately shaped by cost factors, zoning laws, and building codes. Two sets of New York zoning laws —1916 and 1961—resulted in two characteristic building types: the ziggurat setbacks produced by the earlier law and the blocky base and shaft or the free-standing tower of the revised version.

1. Hugh Ferriss study for the maximum mass permitted by the 1916 New York zoning law.
2. 1916-style ziggurat next to 1961-style setbacks.
3. Zoning contrasts.

and flagrantly abused, and is so abusive of everything around it.

Cities like New York, synonymous with the big building, encourage their own exploitation. In recent years, New York has been aiding and abetting more massive construction than that which sparked the horrified reaction that led to the original zoning restrictions of 1916. This unprecedented building size stems from the 1960 revision of the zoning law, which encouraged the tall tower surrounded by open space, an ideal that had long been the modernists' dream. A series of innovative bonuses and special permits were devised for the provision of public features such as plazas and arcades. This kind of incentive zoning, which had many admirable urbanistic objectives, including the preservation of theaters and neighborhoods, was skillfully manipulated by builders and their lawyers. Its subjective, permissive approach encouraged speculation, which led to inflated land values, which, in turn, required ever larger structures; this was followed by claims of economic hardship due to high land prices and requests for variances for still larger buildings. It is Catch-22 at the highest exploitative level. The city presides over this blockbuster zoning-roulette in a planning charade, routinely endorsing the pop-up Frankenstein towers after a ritual display of concern and compromise; they continue to be built to a scale New York has never known or sanctioned before. Many of these outrageous projects are "sweetened" by big architectural names.

Recent downzoning in midtown Manhattan has been aimed at correcting the most obvious abuses, but even with the cutbacks the buildings still allowed are bigger than those permitted by earlier laws. And the revisions often rely on a clever shuffle of sun-and-shadow criteria using calculations so complex that only a computer can deal with them. In a kind of fast-building monte, or architectural shell game, being played from East Side to West, the offending densities are shifted from one part of town to another, overpowering each area in turn. Residential neighborhoods, still overzoned, remain open season for developers; every avenue bears a mysterious set of zoning numbers that permits gross increases in size. The destructive aspects of this kind of zoning have no computer calculations, only human ones.

Do the arguments of economic development justify this degree of overbuilding? Is there a line where economic destiny can no longer be distinguished from pure greed? Is the famous skyline enough? At what point do the urban and cultural assets that are the city's great draw lose out to a painful and abrasive and underserviced environment? At what moment does the city cross that line where it ceases to be magnificent and becomes insupportable? Can a city invite its own decline?

Finally, how much, if any, of this must the architect answer for? New York's bumper crop of new skyscrapers vie with each other in the uniqueness of their design, as well as in their shattering scale. Other cities follow where New York leads in architectural excess. After many years of New York–watching, and many battles with developers dedicated to the lowest formula of commercial design, one must come to the reluctant conclusion that at this level of overbuilding and its attendant problems, aesthetics cancel out. Architecture simply doesn't count.

As an observer and critic devoted to the quality of art and life, I never thought that I would make that statement. It is particularly ironic to have to make it now, in view of the fact that these blockbusters are among the best of the breed ever built in New York. With pitifully few exceptions in the past, New York's skyscrapers have never reached for anything but money. Many of these new buildings are the work of architects of reputation. But to anyone who believes that functions of density and amenity are germane to the art of architecture—that what buildings do is as critical as how they look—these structures make architecture unimportant and even meaningless. And the effete stylistic debates about them make architecture ludicrous. To judge these buildings in aesthetic terms is absurd.

In New York, the impact of these concentrated superskyscrapers on street scale and sunlight, on the city's antiquated support systems, circulation, and infrastructure, on its already tenuous livability, overrides any aesthetic. As bulk and density increase, avenues darken and close in; shadows lengthen and downdrafts multiply; winter sun becomes a fleeting penetration of cold canyons at midday, leaving neither warmth nor cheer. The city's oppressive impersonality increases, while services suffer and civility diminishes; amenities disappear or are traded off for questionable substitutes. Architecture, in this context, is only a game architects play. Art becomes worthless in a city brutalized by overdevelopment.

The last to know, or admit, this are the architects themselves. They are offering us a select-a-style skyline, as if that were the only thing that mattered. They keep company with city officials who see nothing but the beauties of the tax base and lawyers devoted to the aesthetics of the legal loophole. Developers are congenitally incapable of thinking of anything except the art of maximized profit; it is only New York's boom-and-bust construction cycles that have traditionally kept them from destroying both the goose and the golden egg.

Meanwhile, the architects are having a wonderful time rearranging the deck chairs on the *Titanic*. Some, of course, are building these behemoths, and others are composing panegyrics to the latest fashion in historical allusionism, as they previously composed them to the most recent technological innovation. Pick your rationale; it really doesn't matter for these cash-flow monuments.

The evidence is overwhelming in the rebuilding of Madison Avenue between Fiftieth and Sixtieth Streets,

Revisions of New York's 1961 zoning have produced not smaller buildings, or buildings with better public manners, but, perversely, bigger and bulkier buildings than before. The impact of the blockbuster skyscrapers of the 1980s can be seen in the blocks from Fifty-Fifth to Fifty-Seventh Streets on Madison and Fifth Avenues.

1. The enormous bulk and overscaled architecture of the AT&T building by the firm of Johnson, Burgee (1978–83) is more notable for its gross, heavy-handed assault on Madison Avenue than for its well-publicized Chippendale top.

2. The IBM building by Edward L. Barnes Associates (1977–83), at the same preposterous scale, attempts to ameliorate its bulk by conscious design devices—a skilled exercise in futility.

3. The Trump tower, by Der Scutt with the firm of Swanke, Hayden, and Connell (1979–83), an immense, faceted form that could be appropriately dramatic somewhere else, compounds the concentrated errors and abuses of planning, zoning, and design.

2

3

where an appalling concentration of new superskyscrapers makes pre-1916 Wall Street and post–World War II midtown look picturesque. It also makes the city's zoning look like a bad joke. This is exactly the kind of construction, with its deleterious side effects, that zoning was devised to prevent, and the realization of what the New York zoning has wrought has led to public protest and some midtown revisions.

Philip Johnson is right when he says that the controversial pediment-top of his AT&T building between Fifty-Fifth and Fifty-Sixth Streets is unimportant; what counts is the way the structure's enormous bulk and pretentious, overblown detail have finally shaped up as a heavy-handed assault on the avenue. This building cannot even be seen by the person on the street below it, short of his lying down in a hole bored in the base of a building across the way. Its block-long, crushing descent to the sidewalk is relentlessly brutal; not only does its size flout the urban and civic intent of restrictive zoning, but its siting fails utterly to provide the sight lines essential to a work of architecture. This fact is not redeemed by an imperial colonnade at ground level or by oversized oculi that make the understanding of the subtle and powerful uses of the void in a solid wall of Renaissance and classical masters all too clear by contrast. Whatever their vaunted mannerisms, these are just big holes.

The IBM building on the next block, between Fifty-Sixth and Fifty-Seventh Streets, by Edward L. Barnes and Associates, is built to the same preposterous scale. But here the architect has attempted to accommodate the impossible and the undesirable with notable skill, something that gives Barnes the dubious distinction of at least trying to do the wrong thing right. IBM's taut, refined skin of granite and glass upstages AT&T like a suave fashion model next to a fussy dowager in a homemade dress. The extravagantly cantilevered corner that frees the sidewalk and the diagonal slice that reveals the sky and slims the building's huge bulk afford some trompe l'oeil relief from its overwhelming mass.

The difference in the two buildings—IBM is by far the better one—is the demonstrable way in which the design process gives meaning to idea and purpose. AT&T's ideas are as thin as its borrowed symbols are large; this super-pastiche relates to nothing except its own overbearing aspirations. Although IBM is plainer, it is richer in its concern with urban relationships and its immediate world; it sets up tensions and responses of far greater architectural inferences and rewards. The choice of a modernist or postmodernist style is quite beside the point, although it is clear that IBM handles its vocabulary with infinitely more ease. What matters is making architecture out of it, and whether architecture applies here at all.

One block west, Der Scutt has created the gigantic Trump tower, a soaring, faceted form that is also guaranteed to destroy the scale and ambience of Fifth Avenue. This dubious achievement has already been demonstrated by Olympic tower, one of the first structures to zap the Avenue by taking advantage of the massive zoning packages that could be put together by an astute builder. Trump tower might be an interesting design somewhere else; here it is totally out of place. Its unexceptionally detailed, dark glass skin is dull and ordinary, and the pink marble maelstrom and pricey superglitz of the shopping atrium are unredeemed by the posh ladies' room decor. It bears no relationship to the quiet limestone facades and traditional worldly elegance of Fifth Avenue that it so aggressively aspires to, qualities epitomized by that earlier Fifth Avenue skyscraper complex, Rockefeller Center. Trump and his architect should have looked south.

What all of these oversized buildings in close proximity will contribute to density and gridlock is anyone's guess. But their damage to the city's comfort and character, their threat to its convenience, mobility, and existential pleasures, is already apparent. The zoning trade-off for so much increased bulk and height is the windswept plaza and the public passageway; some add to the city, some do not. These spaces occasionally ameliorate the disadvantages of high density, but they never justify it; they range from the highly debatable asset of a fancier building lobby, a few of which really offer pleasant places to sit, to generously landscaped street plazas. IBM's space-frame enclosure could be the optimum example of the indoor garden, but the tubing of the frame lacks the delicacy suggested by the early models, and the bamboo trees fail to hold their own against it. City gardens require lavish, rather than restrained, planting. If Trump tower revels in an absence of refinement, IBM suffers from too much.

In the end, the zoning trade-offs have become their own reward. The balance between the mandated amenity and sanctioned overbuilding operates with the kind of grotesque logic with which compromises of public purpose are lobbied through the urban political shoals.

Broadway Boogie-Woogie

The redevelopment of Broadway's tawdry and tarnished Times Square is a case history of the process by which the outrageous becomes standard. It also demonstrates how political infighting and high economic stakes can turn a good plan into a bad one. What was originally a sensitive response to the needs and character of the area ended as a sanitized exercise in upscale skyscraper real estate.

The Times Square Redevelopment Plan was conceived as a city-state effort to reclaim the severely blighted Forty-Second Street block between Seventh and Eighth Avenues from its long, sordid decline, as part of the revitalization of the legendary Crossroads of the World and Great White Way. New office construction was to introduce a healthier and more profitable working population, at the same time that the area's important role as a tourist and entertainment center was to be maintained and reinforced. The historic Forty-Second Street theaters were to be restored.

After careful study, a set of design guidelines was prepared to control the nature of the tall buildings in order to meet these objectives; the guidelines became a contractual part of the developer's package. The developer selected for the new Times Square office buildings (separate parts of the plan dealt with saving the theaters, building a merchandise mart, and upgrading the subway) was George Klein of Park Tower Realty; he chose the architectural firm of John Burgee Architects with Philip Johnson.

The four proposed towers were very large; their size was calculated, in part, to create a financial spinoff that would help pay for the restoration of the old theaters. The official guidelines for these towers were specific: they were to be given a special "Times Square" image through the use of clear, light, sparkling, or shining materials; open and welcoming ground floors were to stress visibility and activity. Setbacks were defined and specified to lessen the buildings' bulk and to insure sight lines and sun. The famous lighted signs were to be part of the overall plan, and so was the Times tower, which was to be retained as symbol and landmark, although it had been badly mutilated by an earlier remodeling. The architects were given total flexibility for its treatment. The guidelines stressed the uniqueness and importance of the area; they also encouraged a dynamic ensemble.

With a change in the state administration, the agency in charge, the New York State Urban Development Corporation, was reshuffled, and a different set of signals came from Albany and City Hall. The requirements could be played down or compromised as long as a "world-class" development resulted. Two years after the publication of the guidelines, a monstrous scheme was unveiled at a press conference in which city and state officials jostled for place and vied in the enthusiasm of their endorsement. The plan called for surrounding Times Square with a formal phalanx of enormous, identical blockbusters, without the required setbacks, lacking the specified lightness and openness, and minus a Times tower, which the developer and architects planned to demolish because it interfered with their clear preference for investment and aesthetic unity. The bland, redundant rhythms of the overscaled and monotonously pilastered ground floors would have pleased Armando Brasini or Albert Speer. The towers wore fancy hats with spikes as a gesture to New York's turn-of-the-century mansards. At least one of them, larger than anything previously permitted by the city's zoning, made the towers of the past look puny.

That part of the guidelines with the greatest importance for the architectural and urban character of the area had simply been thrown away. Even with the tremendous financial advantages of land assembly and tax abatements being given to ease the pain of following the specifications, no concessions had been made.

Some signs and decorative lights were added when protests from civic groups mounted; since they are not intrinsic to the design, they can just as easily be removed. What the developer clearly wanted was an expensive, élite corporate image, with rentals and views to match. He and his architects spoke of creating a new Rockefeller Center; critics noted that the objective was not a new Rockefeller Center but a new Times Square.

The Forty-Second Street plan is a throwback to urban renewal in its most sterile, insensitive, hackneyed, and discredited form; it is as if the hard lessons of recent decades about the interaction of buildings, people, and cities had never been learned. Times Square's image and role in the city's history were completely ignored as a source and function of the new design. But the most disturbing lesson, which occurs over and over in the annals of city planning, is the fact that enough time had elapsed, and enough speculation and development had started on the midtown West Side, to raise serious questions about the need for the financial and urban giveaway and the impact of this inhumane scheme on the area's density and character.

At the same time that the New York skyscraper was taking a giant step backward, competitors in the Soling Architecture Student Design Competition, sponsored by the Syracuse University School of Architecture, were unveiling their ideas of the tall building's future. This intercollegiate project of 1983 brought entries from

At this massive scale, redevelopment plans for Times Square exchange its tawdry glitter and tarnished history for a monolithic, monotonous scheme as lifeless as any of the discredited urban renewals of the 1960s. Like them, this 1983 version is meant to clear out blight and jack up the area's economic base. But the stark, bottom-line boxes favored twenty years ago have been replaced by equally static buildings of homogenized, quasi-traditional pseudo-grandeur. The formal eclecticism of the matched set of towers by John Burgee Architects with Philip Johnson, shown here in the model, is clearly considered a more desirable investment image than any kind of razzle-dazzle; the design suggests upscale rentals. The lessons learned about the life and character of special places have been discarded; the substitute is a thin veneer of a marketable style.

Syracuse, Harvard, Yale, Cornell, the University of Virginia, Cooper Union, the Rhode Island School of Design, and the Institute for Architecture and Urban Studies in New York. The detailed competition instructions called for a high-rise, mixed-use building to contain a theater, offices, and a hotel on a 38,000-square-foot site on Broadway between Fifty-Second and Fifty-Third Streets; the problem had more than a casual conceptual link with the Times Square plan.

But this was no ordinary student exercise; the most important, and fundamental, requirement was compliance with New York's building and zoning codes. Indoctrination included a seminar in New York and a project advisor from the New York City Planning Commission. Explicitly, the assignment was meant to test the city's newly revised midtown zoning and the students' responses to it. Implicitly, the problem addressed was one of the style and character of the tall building in a specific context, as well as of its physical and economic viability—substantially the same conditions that had motivated the creation of the Times Square guidelines.

The imaginative variety and creative excellence of the student solutions leave the Times Square towers far behind. All of the competition designs were judged structurally feasible; most passed building code and service system review; two-thirds fulfilled the zoning requirements. A first prize was awarded to Richard Cook and Peter Wiederspahn of Syracuse and second

prize went to Kevin Havens of Harvard; both came through on every count. A special merit award, given to Frank Lupo of Yale, was substituted for a third prize because his scheme fell short of zoning compliance but was impressive enough to be recognized.

These designs make it clear that a conventional New York zoning configuration of base and shaft can be enlivened by the imaginative handling of the relationship of facade to functions. The effective treatment of entrances and ground floor commercial uses in Kevin Havens's scheme displays a competence barely hinted at by the outer-space image, which is actually closer to early, revolutionary Russian Constructivism than to science fiction. The structure's eloquent and convincing theatricality seems both suitable and appealing for the site. "The building is about the energy of Broadway," Havens has explained. "It channels that energy, takes it up from the street, up through the shaft, and explodes it at the top, making that energy visible on the skyline." How much more appropriate a response to the city's unique creative challenge than historical charades and aesthetic dandyism!

This work is already beyond postmodernist debate; it demonstrates the ease with which today's young professionals have absorbed an unprecedented range of source material unavailable to the Beaux Arts—trained or modernist-educated practitioner. They have developed the skills to integrate these sources into a new vocabulary, or vocabularies; recognizing the limitations

What may be the skyscraper of the future is appearing now in the work and dreams of younger architects; some of the most interesting and prophetic possibilities came out of a 1983 intercollegiate student competition sponsored by Syracuse University. The projects were for a Broadway site similar in nature to Times Square. Although the program required detailed compliance with New York's zoning and building codes, the results, as shown in these models, were marked by a variety, boldness, and remarkable professional skill that make the Times Square towers pale. The clear conviction emerges that a new order, or orders, have been born. If super-buildings threaten the virtues and pleasures of urban life, these studies suggest that the city will destroy itself in a blaze of invention. The search for the ultimate skyscraper goes on.

1. *First prize, Richard Cook and Peter Wiederspahn of Syracuse University.*
2. *Second prize, Kevin Havens of Harvard University.*

3

4

3. *Special merit award, Frank Lupo of Yale University.*
4. *Honorable mention, Thomas Peterman of Harvard University.*
5. *Honorable mention, Mark Weintraub and David Bushnell of Cornell University.*
6. *Citation, Craig Konyk of the University of Virginia.*

5

6

of architecture as a sociological tool, they deal with the tall building in a more specific cultural and environmental context. A dramatic range of practical and expressive possibilities is beginning to emerge.

The Superskyscraper

Admittedly, the tall building works dramatically well for business and its satellite services; to deny this fact and its corollary, that the development of the skyscraper has logically served these characteristically twentieth-century needs, is to miss the real nature of our civilization and of the most conspicuous architecture of our time. The validity of the symbolism of the tall building for its age is intrinsic to its powerful imagery. Its single historical consistency has been its predictable penchant for setting records, for rising to ever greater heights. A group of distinguished skyscraper architects and engineers met to discuss this phenomenon in a symposium on "Supertall Buildings," sponsored by the editors of a leading professional publication, *The Engineering News-Record*, in 1983.

Five of the participants were in the process of designing some version of the world's tallest building. At least three had already developed superskyscrapers in anticipation of demand. The Chicago architect, Harry Weese, with the help of the New York engineering firm of Lev Zetlin, was ready with a 210-story structure using a twisted shaft of superior strength and wind resistance based on the principle of a tower held by guy

wires. Robert Sobel of the New York architectural firm of Emery Roth and Sons, working with the Rice University engineer Nat Krahl, had tested a bundled-tube design for Houston, in which a cluster of attached shafts can "bundle" their strength and rigidity to rise as high as a theoretical 500 stories. The engineer Hal Iyengar, of Skidmore, Owings, and Merrill, was ready with a telescoped-truss "superframe" for a building in the 150-to-200-story range. The superskyscraper loomed over the horizon. (Not long after, one of New York's less reticent developers, Donald Trump, proposed to pursue the world's-tallest-building title with a 150-story tower for lower Manhattan.)

If there was no lack of assurance about the structural engineers' ability to build higher, there was considerably less confidence in the development of the necessary service technologies required to make these buildings function. The elevators for a 200-story structure would have to be equivalent to a light rail system serving a vertical city, something beyond the current state of the art. The delivery of water and energy would bring problems of excessive hydrostatic pressure and enormous heating and cooling tasks; these buildings would need their own electrical substations. Safety requirements at 200 stories would automatically make existing fire and other codes obsolete. The problems of supertall buildings, it was pointed out, have little to do with beauty or the forces of gravity. They have everything to do with the peculiarities of a structure's dynamic behavior as its size increases; wind, for example, is a more serious and constant factor than earthquakes.

Other questions were raised: What about deepening shadows; the hostile microclimate at the supertall building's base; traffic, parking, and loading problems; the skewing of the city's functions and services that a single supertall structure could cause? The jump from 100 to 200 stories does not just double calculations and difficulties; engineers must deal with what they call "exaggerated multiples of behavior." Theoretically, for example, the total volume of traffic will vary as a cube of the height, so that doubling the building's height increases the traffic volume eight times. Superbuildings like the 110-story twin towers of New York's World Trade Center bring Superbowl crowds—50,000 employees and 80,000 visitors every day. Ground space and transit become critical factors.

Then why go taller? Because, said engineer Vincent DeSimone, heroic structures capture the public's imagination and clients are intensely competitive. Ego is going to drive the next building higher. "There are no limits," said Paul Weidlinger, who has engineered some of the biggest. "We always do what has to be done, and that is what makes engineering interesting." Without the right investment figures, Robert Sobel pointed out, you can forget ego trips and the engineering challenges of the superbuilding. "I think there are financial forces working to make this happen." It was unanimously agreed that records are made to be broken.

But if supertall buildings can be designed and built, and probably will be, there was no consensus that they are desirable. Architect Eugene Kohn—whose firm, Kohn, Pedersen, Fox, seems to get skyscraper commissions weekly—observed that the engineering technology that makes them possible has far outstripped human responses or the ability to cope with or enjoy the results. Although twentieth-century dams, bridges, and buildings have reshaped the natural and man-made worlds, the results have not always been predictable or benign. As Paul Weidlinger observed, "Heroic problems require heroic engineering solutions; the engineering solutions, in turn, produce heroic social problems."

Those problems are increasingly apparent. We still lack a realistic understanding of the physical connections and limitations of a built environment on this scale. Architectural concentrations of such size require a proper municipal infrastructure and support services; they also need the kind of practical and conceptual planning that is very much out of fashion right now. And while today's tolerance of variety and incremental change is desirable and necessary—modernism's blindness on this score is one of its most vulnerable points—the current trendy ad-hoc-ism is not enough. "The idea that a single individual should be allowed to make all these decisions privately is absurd," said William Le Messurier, one of the most experienced skyscraper engineers. "We wouldn't let anybody do a dam that might flood a city by himself, or design a nuclear plant by himself—why a 200-story building?" When buildings go higher, the public stakes go higher. There is no harmless contextualism in the development world; there is only aggressive and exploitative change.

The Critical Challenges

As for the stylistic changes that are the current focus of attention, Montgomery Schuyler's observation of 1899 is still valid. "It all depends," he wrote, "on whether the departure is a mere caprice of the designer, or an attempt to come closer to reason and reality." Today's architecture has moved dangerously close to mere caprice. But the design process has also become much more diverse and open, with all that this implies of creativity and abuse. Today there are equal opportunities for poetic license and architectural malpractice. With this new freedom, the possibilities for good and bad building are as spectacular as some of the new structures.

The architectural historian, accustomed to the long view, sees this moment as neither heresy nor revelation; change is the natural creative order. It is a moment of discovery, testing, and transition. Unfortunately, Schuyler's "reason and reality" have never been in shorter supply. Significant architectural changes, those real revolutions in perception and practice that are the highpoints of human experience—and that are the real sources of style—are being subverted by a public and profession more addicted to publicity and novelty than to reason and reality. A lot of fashionable intellectual underbrush that needs clearing out is hopelessly confusing the rational priorities of a utilitarian structural art.

If architecture cannot be judged as a beauty contest, the issues to be addressed are, at best, difficult and unclear. Nothing about architecture, which must serve many masters, is simple. The difficult dynamics of utility and beauty, of poetry and pragmatism, those rational and spiritual components that are in perpetual conflict, defy definitive resolution; in fact, they resist resolution at all. There is no unflawed building. There is no perfect answer, no exemplary balance, no replicable typology; it is the very essence of the building art to have changing meanings and irreconcilable demands. The practical and aesthetic accommodations of architecture must always be partial, incomplete, and subject to redefinitions of need and taste.

The rigorously sensitive kind of design required to fuse function and expression—the pivotal subject addressed in Sullivan's article—is always in flux. The dilemma is faced anew by every architect. The attempt to resolve the conflict—to turn the dilemma into art—has always charged the architectural act with its particular creative energies. This tension, and the degree to which it is directed and controlled, is a significant source of architectural invention and vitality. The process of resolution has produced the most interesting and inspired solutions, and will continue to do so. It is this difficult process that is at the very heart of style—any style. It must be addressed in any valid assessment of quality or success.

The critical challenge of the growing conflict between art and engineering in the nineteenth century was evaded by treating only public and academic architecture as art. The modernist revolution reversed this judgment; the highest respect was reserved for works of pure engineering. Oddly enough, in the twentieth century, the profession entered a gentlemen's agreement not to deal with critical issues at all. "Ethical codes" that never existed before made it improper for architects to evaluate each other's work, even when it involved questions of the public interest. Most professional publications became vehicles of publicity rather than of analysis. (In the predecessors of these periodicals, nineteenth-century architects had engaged in lusty debate.) The substitute for critical debate in this century has been commentary as an instrument of evangelical reform and conversion to modernist doctrine. Only a few superb scholarly observers with a very special vision—Lewis Mumford, Henry-Russell Hitchcock, and Nikolaus Pevsner—managed both the call to conversion and the need for critical evaluation with distinction and grace.

In recent years, a floodgate of architectural writing has opened, but much of it is a pretentious, debased, and discursive product that fails to come to terms with the hard facts of the art. At the moment when the skyscraper has entered a radical stage of its stylistic development, it is being viewed in the narrowest, shallowest, and most disappointing terms as a purely hedonistic or titillating visual object. It is increasingly seen as something "to massage the eye." Alas, the eye is being assaulted as much as it is being massaged, and the two are frequently indistinguishable—a phenomenon that is probably legitimately reflective of the current emphasis on transient massages, or messages, of all kinds.

If the modern skyscraper has resolved any of architecture's intrinsic ambiguities, it has done so in a thoroughly unexpected and unsettling way. Today's big building is a masterpiece of economic manipulation, a monument to the marketplace and entrepreneurial skills. These are skills that command the kind of reverence and awe reserved for theological, moral, and aesthetic issues in earlier societies. They are given the respect once accorded to matters of the spirit, character, and certain shared, and even ennobling, public values. Those who deal in such financial legerdemain are aware that one of the timeless attributes of architecture is the ability to produce images of identity and status that can contribute to today's profitable package. Whether this is cynicism or realism is not important; what matters is that it puts the practitioner of the art of architecture well below the master of financial leverage in the contemporary hagiography.

The architect who reads the creative script in this limited and ultimately demeaning way may have found a fast track to success. The writer who accepts the formula with no response to its ironies and perversions, with no sense that anything of value is being lost or corrupted, serves no useful function. When praise is given for good intentions that are indistinguishable from exploitation, however good or bad the results, then criticism has been coopted as surely as architecture. The ultimate issues of design quality, the pressing questions of overdevelopment, the relationship of buildings to the people and cultures they serve, the man-made world in all of its unsavory aspects and unrealized potential, are subjects rarely raised. There is art, and the betrayal of art, in all of them. Given the mandate to mutilate or destroy, he who hesitates loses the commission. But the minor arty or intellectual role that the profession is promoting for itself today to the accompaniment of endless, arcane chatter is a kind of self-inflicted architectural castration.

The critic is neither friend nor foe of the architect or builder; he cannot be the apostle of accommodation. He must be both activist and aesthete. The skyscraper, that unique celebration of secular capitalism and its values, challenges us on every level. It offers unique opportunities for insightful analysis in the broadest terms of twentieth-century art, humanity, and history. When criticism becomes captive to centers of power or prevailing theories or fashions, unwilling or unable to probe the process and the results, something important has gone wrong with one of the stabilizing and balancing forces of a mature society.

In the meantime, our old cities are savage and deteriorating, and our new cities are ignoring the lessons of the past and the needs of the future, even as familiar problems begin to sabotage their shortlived, utopian ideals. While this apocalyptic urban script is played out, the search for the ultimate skyscraper goes on. The fact that the focus and objective of the search are narrowing as the size and impact of these buildings increase to record levels is a serious cause for unease— for cities and for architecture alike. At worst, overbuilding will make urban life unbearable. At best, we will go out in a blaze of style.

Picture Sources

Grateful acknowledgment is made to the following for permission to use their photographs:

Eli Attia Architects: page 59 right (photo credit: Michael Zenreich)

Chicago Historical Society: page 42 right (artist: Gilbert Hall)

Cooper-Hewitt Museum: page 103 (courtesy of the Cooper-Hewitt Museum)

Foster Associates: page 88 (photo credit: Richard Davies)

Hedrich-Blessing: pages 19 right, 41 top, 58 right

Gerald D. Hines Interests: pages 67 right, 71 right

Holabird and Root, Architects: pages 15 left, 79 left (credit: Chicago Historical Society)

Wolfgang Hoyt: page 106 (© Wolfgang Hoyt/ESTO)

Humana Inc.: pages 21 left, 90, 91, 92

Garth Huxtable: pages 16, 17, 27, 28, 31 right, 33, 34, 42 left, 43, 44, 47 left, 49, 52, 53, 54, 55, 58 left, 100, 101, 103 top and bottom right

Kohn Pedersen Fox Associates: pages 73 (photo credit: Barbara Karant); 74, 75 right, 76 (photo credit: Jack Horner); 75 left (photo credit: Dan Cornish); 95 left (photo credit: Jack Pottle)

Nathaniel Lieberman: page 111 (© Nathaniel Lieberman)

Murphy, Jahn: pages 21 right, 79, 80, 81 left, 94 (photo credit: Keith Palmer and James Steinkamp); 81 right (photo credit: Doug Hill)

Museum of Modern Art: page 40 left (Mies van der Rohe, Ludwig. Friedrichstrasse Office Building. Berlin. Project, 1921. Perspective. Charcoal and pencil on brown paper mounted to board: 68¼" x 48". Collection, Mies van der Rohe Archive, gift of Ludwig Mies van der Rohe); 50 left (Mies van der Rohe, Ludwig. Concrete Office Building Project. 1922. Exterior perspective. Charcoal, crayon on brown paper: 54½" x 9' 5¹³⁄₁₆". Collection, Mies van der Rohe Archive, Gift of Ludwig Mies van der Rohe)

Richard Nickel Committee: page 31 left

Richard Payne: pages 20, 57, 66, 67 left, 68 (© Richard Payne AIA)

I. M. Pei and Partners: page 59 left (photo credit: Kouo Shang-wei)

Cesar Pelli and Associates: pages 61 (photo credit: David Leonard), 87 upper left (photo credit: Paul Warchol), 87 lower left and upper right (photo credit: Kenneth Champlin Photos)

Cervin Robinson: page 107 left (© Cervin Robinson)

Roche, Dinkeloo, and Associates: page 71 left

Der Scutt: page 107 right (photo credit: Norman McGrath)

Skidmore, Owings, and Merrill: page 95 right (photo credit: © Joe Aker)

Soling Competition, Syracuse University, School of Architecture: pages 113, 114, 115

Ezra Stoller/ESTO: pages 18, 41 bottom, 51, 60 left and bottom (© ESTO)

Harry Weese and Associates: page 60

Lawrence S. Williams, Inc.: page 47 right

Some of the photographs and drawings are in the public domain; some are owned or were provided by someone other than the artist. Photographers who could be identified are:

Jack Boucher: page 30
Alexandre Georges: page 40 right

Index

Page numbers in italic refer to illustrations.

About the Author

Ada Louise Huxtable, architecture critic of the *New York Times* from 1963 to 1982 and a member of its editorial board from 1973 to 1982, was the first full-time critic in this field on an American newspaper. She left the *Times* after she was named a MacArthur Prize Fellow in December 1981. The winner of the first Pulitzer Prize for Distinguished Criticism in 1970, she has received over thirty other professional awards as well as over twenty-five honorary degrees. In addition to *The Tall Building Artistically Reconsidered*, she is the author of *Pier Luigi Nervi*, a study of the Italian engineer; *Classical New York*; *Will They Ever Finish Bruckner Boulevard?* and *Kicked a Building Lately?*